coding
PROJECTS
IN SCRATCH™

coding PROJECTS IN SCRATCH™

JON WOODCOCK

DK UK

Senior editor Ben Morgan
Project editor Ben Ffrancon Davies
Senior art editor Jacqui Swan
US editor Jennette ElNaggar
Consultant editor Craig Steele
Jacket design development manager Sophia MTT
Jacket editor Emma Dawson
Jacket designer Surabhi Wadhwa
Producer, pre-production Gillian Reid
Senior producers Meskerem Berhane, Mary Slater
Managing editor Lisa Gillespie
Managing art editor Owen Peyton Jones
Publisher Andrew Macintyre
Associate publishing director Liz Wheeler
Art director Karen Self
Design director Phil Ormerod
Publishing director Jonathan Metcalf

DK INDIA

Senior editor Suefa Lee
Project editor Tina Jindal
Project art editors Sanjay Chauhan, Parul Gambhir
Editor Sonia Yooshing
Art editors Rabia Ahmad, Simar Dhamija, Sonakshi Singh
Jacket designers Priyanka Bansal, Suhita Dharamjit
Jackets editorial coordinator Priyanka Sharma
Managing jackets editor Saloni Singh
DTP designers Jaypal Singh Chauhan, Rakesh Kumar
Senior managing editor Rohan Sinha
Managing art editor Sudakshina Basu
Pre-production manager Balwant Singh

This American Edition, 2019
First American Edition, 2016
Published in the United States by DK Publishing
1745 Broadway, 20th Floor, New York, NY 10019

Copyright © 2016, 2019 Dorling Kindersley Limited
DK, a Division of Penguin Random House LLC
23 24 25 26 10 9 8 7 6 5 4 3 2
010–291611–Aug/2019

A catalog record for this book is available from the Library of Congress.
ISBN 978-1-4654-7734-7

DK books are available at special discounts when purchased in bulk for sales promotions, premiums, fund-raising, or educational use. For details, contact: DK Publishing Special Markets, 1745 Broadway, 20th Floor, New York, NY 10019
SpecialSales@dk.com

Printed and bound in China

www.dk.com

This book was made with Forest Stewardship Council™ certified paper – one small step in DK's commitment to a sustainable future.
For more information go to
www.dk.com/our-green-pledge

DR. JON WOODCOCK MA (OXON) has a degree in physics from the University of Oxford and a PhD in computational astrophysics from the University of London. He started coding at the age of eight and has programmed all kinds of computers, from single-chip microcontrollers to world-class supercomputers. His many projects include giant space simulations, research in high-tech companies, and intelligent robots made from junk. Jon has a passion for science and technology education, giving talks on space and running computer programming clubs in schools. He has worked on numerous science and technology books as a contributor and consultant, including DK's *Computer Coding for Kids* and *Computer Coding Made Easy* and DK's series of coding workbooks.

CRAIG STEELE is a specialist in computing science education who helps people develop digital skills in a fun and creative environment. He is a founder of CoderDojo in Scotland, which runs free coding clubs for young people. Craig has run digital workshops with the Raspberry Pi Foundation, Glasgow Science Centre, Glasgow School of Art, BAFTA, and the BBC micro:bit project. Craig's first computer was a ZX Spectrum.

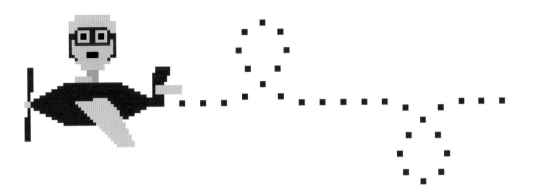

Contents

5 SIMULATIONS

7 MINDBENDERS

6 MUSIC AND SOUND

8 WHAT NEXT?

Find out more at:
www.dk.com/computercoding

Foreword

In recent years, interest in coding has exploded. All over the world, schools are adding coding to their curriculums, code clubs are being launched to teach beginners, and adults are returning to college to learn coding skills now considered vital in the workplace. And in homes everywhere, millions of people are learning how to code just for the fun of it.

Fortunately, there's never been a better time to learn how to code. In the past, programmers had to type out every line of code by hand, using obscure commands and mathematical symbols. A single period out of place could ruin everything. Today, you can build amazingly powerful programs in minutes by using drag-and-drop coding languages like Scratch™, which is used in this book.

As learning to code has become easier, more people have discovered the creative potential of computers, and that's where this book comes in. *Coding Projects in Scratch* is all about using code for creative purposes—to make art, music, animation, and special effects. With a little bit of imagination you can produce dazzling results, from glittering fireworks displays to kaleidoscope-like masterpieces that swirl and beat in time to music.

If you're completely new to coding, don't worry—the first two chapters will walk you through the basics and teach you everything you need to know to use Scratch. The later chapters then build on your skills, showing you how to create interactive artworks, lifelike simulations, mind-bending optical illusions, and some great games.

Learning something new can sometimes feel like hard work, but I believe you learn faster when you're having fun. This book is based on that idea, so we've tried to make it as much fun as possible. We hope you enjoy building the projects in this book as much as we enjoyed making them.

On your mark ...
get set ... CODE!

What is coding?

Creative computers

Computers are everywhere and are used in all sorts of creative ways. But to really join in the fun, you need to take control of your computer and learn how to program it. Programming puts a world of possibilities at your fingertips.

Think like a computer

Programming, or coding, simply means telling a computer what to do. To write a program you need to think like a computer, which means breaking down a task into a series of simple steps. Here's how it works.

▷ **A simple recipe**

Imagine you want a friend to bake a cake, but your friend has no idea how to cook. You can't simply give an instruction like "make a cake"—your friend won't know where to start. Instead, you need to write a recipe, with simple steps like "break an egg," "add the sugar," and so on. Programming a computer is a bit like writing a recipe.

◁ **Step by step**

Now imagine you want to program a computer to create a painting like the one shown here, with colored circles overlapping each other at random. You have to turn the job of painting the picture into a kind of recipe, with steps the computer can follow. It might look something like this:

Recipe

Ingredients

1. Ten circles of various sizes

2. Seven colors

Instructions

1. Clear the screen to create a white background.

2. Repeat the following ten times:

    a) Pick a random place on the screen.

    b) Pick one of the circles randomly.

    c) Pick one of the colors randomly.

    d) Draw a see-through copy of the circle at that place in that color.

▷ **Computer language**

Although you can understand the recipe for a painting or a cake, a computer can't. You need to translate the instructions into a special language that the computer can understand—a programming language. The one used in this book is called Scratch.

Worlds of imagination

There isn't a single creative field in the world that hasn't been touched by computers. In this book, you'll get to make lots of great projects that will fire your imagination and make you think and code creatively.

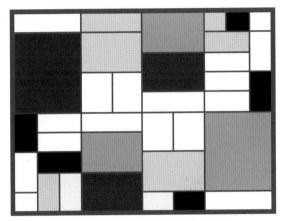

Computers can be programmed to create original works of art.

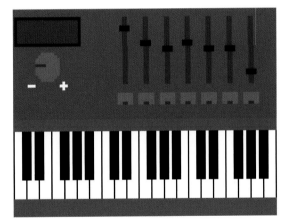

Sound programs can mix musical and other sound effects in any combination.

Building games programs is just as much fun as playing them, especially when you make all the rules.

Special effects and dramatic scenery in movies are often created in graphics programs.

Programming languages

To tell a computer what to do, you need to speak the right kind of language: a programming language. There are lots to choose from, ranging from easy ones for beginners, like the one in this book, to complex languages that take years to master. A set of instructions written in any programming language is called a program.

Popular languages

There are more than 500 different programming languages, but most programs are written in just a handful of these. The most popular languages use English words, but lines of code look very different from English sentences. Here's how to get a computer to say "Hello!" on screen in just a few of today's languages.

Hello!

▷ **C**
The C programming language is often used for code that runs directly on a computer's hardware, such as the Windows operating system. C is good for building software that needs to run fast, and has been used to program space probes.

```
#include <stdio.h>
main(){ printf("Hello!"); }
```

Hello!

▷ **C++**
This complicated language is used to build large, commercial programs such as word processors, web browsers, and operating systems. C++ is based on C, but with extra features that make it better for big projects.

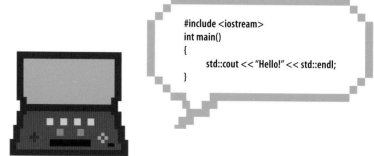

```
#include <iostream>
int main()
{
      std::cout << "Hello!" << std::endl;
}
```

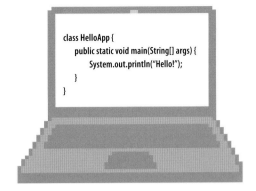

△ Scratch

Beginners often start with simple programming languages such as Scratch. Instead of typing out code, you build scripts with ready-made blocks of code.

△ Java

Java code is designed to work on all types of devices, from cell phones and laptops to games consoles and supercomputers. Minecraft is written in Java.

△ Python

Python is a very popular, all-purpose language. The lines of code are shorter and simpler than in other languages, making it easier to learn. Python is a great language to learn after Scratch.

△ JavaScript

Programmers use JavaScript to create interactive features that run on websites, such as advertisements and games.

▪▪▪ LINGO

Code words

Algorithm A set of instructions that are followed to perform a particular task. Computer programs are based on algorithms.

Bug A mistake in a program. They are called bugs because the first computers had problems when insects got stuck in their circuits.

Code Computer instructions written in a programming language are often called code. Coding is programming.

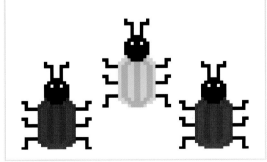

How Scratch works

This book shows you how to build some really cool projects using the Scratch programming language. Programs are made by dragging together ready-made blocks of instruction code to control colorful characters called sprites.

Sprites

Sprites are the objects shown on the screen. Scratch comes with a huge selection of sprites—such as elephants, bananas, and balloons—but you can also draw your own. Sprites can perform all sorts of actions, like moving, changing color, and spinning around.

I'm a sprite!

Sprites can move around.

Sprites can play sounds and music.

Sprites can deliver messages on the screen.

Blocks of code

Scratch's multicolored instruction blocks tell sprites what to do. Each sprite gets its instructions from stacks of Scratch blocks called code blocks. Each instruction block is performed in turn from the top to the bottom. Here's some simple code for this vampire sprite.

▽ **Creating code blocks**
The blocks that make the code are dragged together using a computer mouse. They lock together like pieces of a jigsaw puzzle. Blocks come in color-coded families to help you find the correct block easily. For example, all the purple blocks change a sprite's appearance.

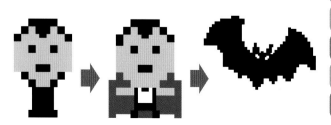

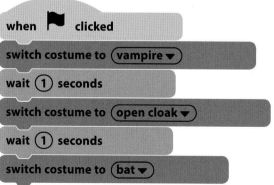

when ⚑ clicked
switch costume to (vampire ▼)
wait (1) seconds
switch costume to (open cloak ▼)
wait (1) seconds
switch costume to (bat ▼)

A typical Scratch project

A Scratch project is made up of sprites, code blocks, and sounds, which work collectively to create action on the screen. The area where you see the action is called the stage. You can add a background picture called a backdrop to the stage.

This icon displays the game in full-screen mode.

▷ **Green for go!**
Starting, or "running," a program brings to life the code you've built. In Scratch, clicking the green flag runs all the code blocks in the project. The red button stops the code so you can continue working on your program.

Starts the project

Stops the project

The stage and lights are part of the backdrop (background picture).

The dancing dinosaurs and ballerina are sprites controlled by their own code blocks.

▽ **Code blocks work together**
A project usually has several sprites, each with one or more code blocks. Each code block creates just a part of the action. This code makes a sprite chase the mouse-pointer around the stage.

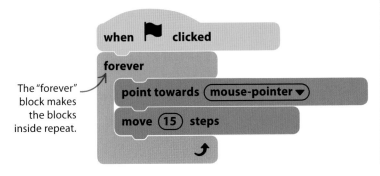

The "forever" block makes the blocks inside repeat.

EXPERT TIPS

Reading Scratch

Scratch is designed to be easily understood. The action performed by each block is written on it, so you can usually figure out what the code does just by reading through it.

Can you guess what this block makes sprites do?

Getting Scratch 3.0

To build the projects in this book and to make your own, you need access to the Scratch 3.0 software on your computer. Just follow these simple instructions.

This book uses Scratch 3.0!

Online and offline Scratch

If your computer is always connected to the internet, it's best to run Scratch online. If not, you need to download and install the offline version.

ONLINE

Visit the Scratch website at **http:// scratch.mit.edu** and click on "Join Scratch" to create an account with a username and password. You'll need an email address, too.

OFFLINE

Visit the Scratch website at **http:// scratch.mit.edu/scratch2download/** and follow the instructions to download and install Scratch on your computer.

Online Scratch runs in your web browser, so just go to the Scratch website and click on "Create" at the top of the screen. The Scratch interface will open.

Scratch will appear as an icon on your desktop, just like any other installed program. Double-click on the Scratch cat icon to get going.

You don't have to worry about saving your work because the online version of Scratch saves projects automatically.

You'll need to save your project by clicking on the File menu and selecting "Save to your computer". Scratch will ask you where to save your work— check with the computer's owner.

Online Scratch should work on Windows, Mac, and Linux computers. This version will also work on tablets.

Offline Scratch works well on Windows and macOS.

Versions of Scratch

The projects in this book need Scratch 3.0 and won't work properly on older versions. If Scratch is already installed on your computer, then consult the pictures below if you're not sure which version it is.

▽ **Scratch 2.0**

In the older version of Scratch, the stage appears on the left. You'll need to install Scratch 3.0.

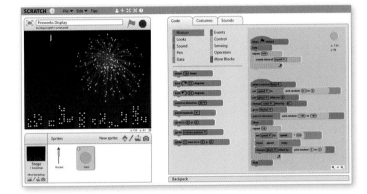

◁ **Scratch 3.0**

In the latest version of Scratch, released in 2019, the stage is on the right, and there are many more blocks and features than in the older versions. Key changes include the addition of new sprites, a better sound editor, and the "Extensions" section, where you can find many new programming blocks.

▪▪▪ EXPERT TIPS

Mouse-pointers

Scratch needs some accurate mouse-work, which is easier to do with a computer mouse than a touch pad. In this book, you'll often be instructed to right-click something with your computer mouse. If your mouse has only one button, you can hold down the shift or control key on your keyboard as you click.

The Scratch interface

This is Scratch mission control. The tools for building code blocks are on the left, while the stage to the right shows you what's going on as your project runs. Don't be afraid to explore!

Select the Code tab to build the code.

Change language

Menu options

Use the Sounds tab to add music and sound effects to sprites.

Use the Costumes tab to change how sprites look.

Blocks palette
Instruction blocks for making code blocks appear on the left of the Scratch window. Drag the ones you want to use to the code area.

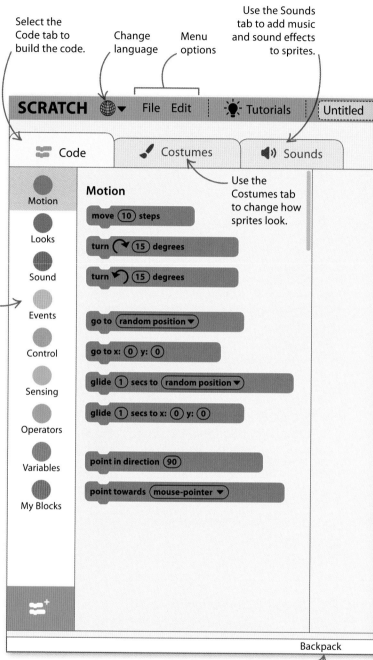

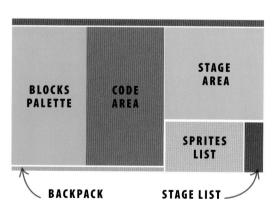

BLOCKS PALETTE
CODE AREA
STAGE AREA
SPRITES LIST

BACKPACK
STAGE LIST

△ **Naming the parts**
While using this book, you'll need to know what's where in the Scratch window. Shown here are the names of the different areas. The tabs above the blocks palette open up other areas of Scratch to edit sounds and sprite costumes.

Backpack
Store useful code blocks, sprites, costumes, and sounds in the backpack so you can use them in other projects.

Code area
Drag blocks into this part of the Scratch window and join them together to build some code for each sprite in your project.

The Stage
This is where the action happens. When you run your project, the stage is where all the sprites appear, moving and interacting as they follow their code blocks.

Click here for a full-screen view of your project.

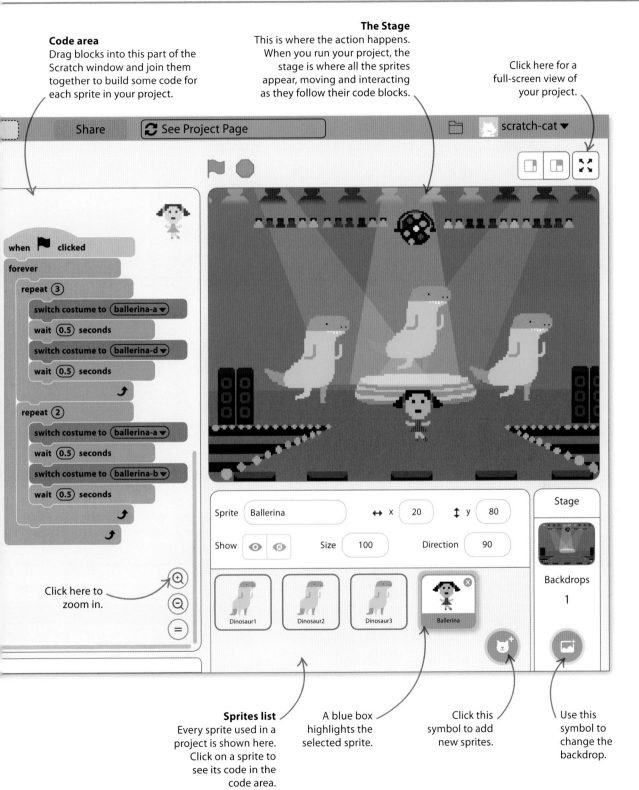

Click here to zoom in.

Sprites list
Every sprite used in a project is shown here. Click on a sprite to see its code in the code area.

A blue box highlights the selected sprite.

Click this symbol to add new sprites.

Use this symbol to change the backdrop.

Types of projects

This book has a wide range of fun Scratch projects. Don't worry if you haven't used Scratch before or you're not an expert—the "Getting started" chapter is there to help you. Here's a handy guide to the projects in this book.

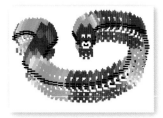
Cat Art (p.26)

Dino Dance Party (p.34)

Animal Race (p.48)

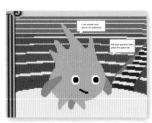
Ask Gobo (p.60)

△ Getting started

Work your way through these easy projects to learn how to use Scratch. Each project introduces important new ideas, so don't skip any if you're a beginner. By the end of the chapter, you'll have mastered the basics of Scratch.

Funny Faces (p.70)

Birthday Card (p.82)

Spiralizer (p.94)

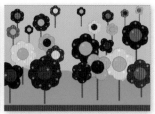
Fantastic Flowers (p.106)

◁ Art

Artists love finding new ways to create art, and computers give them tools that even Leonardo da Vinci couldn't have dreamed of. Make a birthday card, spin spectacular spirals, and cover your world with flowers.

▷ Games

Game design is one of the most creative areas of coding. Game makers are always looking for imaginative new ways to challenge players or tell stories. The projects in this chapter challenge you to steer a sprite through a twisted tunnel or clean virtual splats off a dirty computer screen.

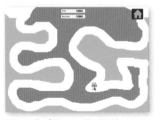
Tunnel of Doom (p.122)

Window Cleaner (p.134)

Virtual Snow (p.144)

Firework Display (p.154)

Fractal Trees (p.162)

Snowflake Simulator (p.172)

△ Simulations

Give a computer the correct information and it can mimic, or simulate, the way things work in the real world. This chapter shows you how to simulate falling snow, sparkling fireworks, the growth of trees, and the shapes of snowflakes.

Sprites and Sounds (p.182)

Drumtastic (p.190)

◁ Music and sound

While early computers struggled to make simple beeps, modern computers can reproduce every instrument in an orchestra. Try out these two treats for your ears. The first one matches sound effects with silly animations, and the second one puts a digital drum kit at your fingertips.

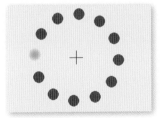
The Magic Spot (p.200)

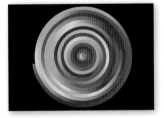
Spiral-o-tron (p.208)

◁ Mindbenders

Making images move in clever ways can fool the eye into seeing amazing patterns and optical illusions. Try these mindbending, spinning-pattern projects.

 **EXPERT TIPS**

Perfect projects

Every project in this book is broken down into easy steps—read each step carefully and you'll sail through them all. The projects tend to get more complicated later in the book. If you find a project isn't doing what it should do, go back a few steps and check the instructions again carefully. If you still have problems, ask an adult to check with you. Once you've got a project working, don't be afraid to change the code and try out your own ideas.

Getting started

Cat Art

Find your feet in Scratch by making some super-simple art with Scratch's cat sprite—the mascot of the Scratch project. This project turns the cat into a kind of multicolored paintbrush. You can use the same trick to paint with any sprite.

Click the green flag to start the project.

Click the stop sign to stop the project.

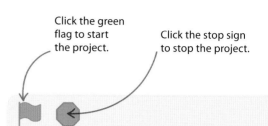

How it works

This simple project lets you use a computer mouse to paint multicolored cat art. Wherever you drag the mouse, a rainbow trail of cats is left behind. Later, you'll see how to add other effects.

△ **Follow the mouse**
First, you'll put together some code to use the mouse-pointer to move the cat sprite around the stage.

△ **Changing color**
Next, you'll add blocks to the code to make the cat change color.

△ **Making copies**
Then, you'll use the "stamp" block to make a trail of copies appear on the stage.

△ **Going wild**
There are lots of crazy effects you can try out on the cat once you start experimenting.

The cat sticks to the mouse-pointer and keeps changing color.

Click here to make the project fill your screen.

◁ **Artistic cat**
This project lets you go wild with your imagination. You can experiment with a variety of colors, sizes, and effects for the cat, and in the end your project will look like a piece of modern art.

Now that's what I call a masterpiece!

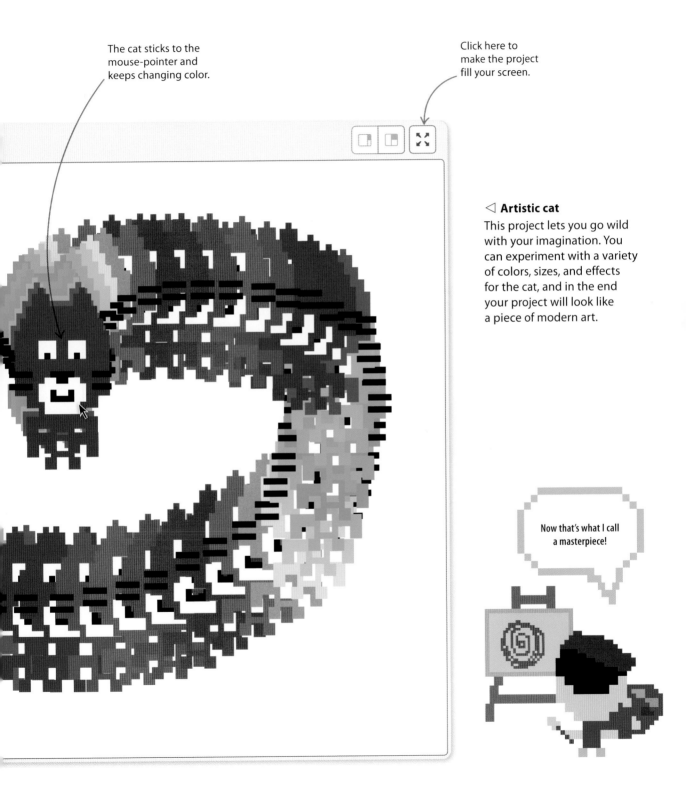

Mouse control

The first step is to make the cat sprite move wherever the mouse-pointer moves. You need to build a set of instructions—called code—to make the cat sprite do this.

Follow me.

1 First, start a new Scratch project. If you use the online version of Scratch, go to the Scratch website and click on Create at the top. If you use Scratch offline, click on the Scratch icon on your desktop. You should see a fresh project, ready for you to start building some code.

The cat sprite on the stage is the only item in a new project.

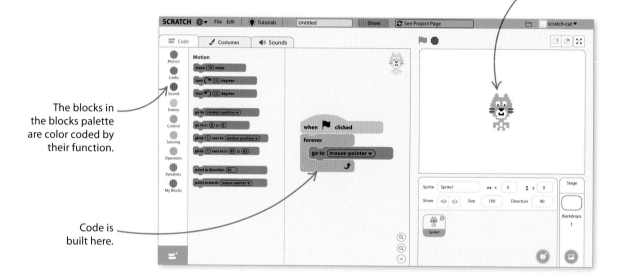

The blocks in the blocks palette are color coded by their function.

Code is built here.

2 To build the code, you simply drag colored blocks from the left (the "blocks palette") to the empty gray space in the middle (the "code area"). The blocks are color coded by what they do. You can switch between different sets of blocks by clicking on the categories at the left of the blocks palette.

Motion is always selected when you start a new project. Clicking on each word shows a different set of colored instruction blocks.

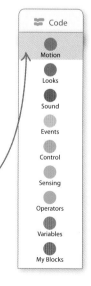

Code

Motion
Looks
Sound
Events
Control
Sensing
Operators
Variables
My Blocks

■ ■ LINGO

Running programs

"Run a program" means "start a program" to a programmer. A program that's doing something is "running." In Scratch, programs are also called projects, and clicking the green flag runs the current project.

3 Select the "go to random position" block and drag it into the code area on the right. It will stay where you put it. Click on the drop-down menu and select "mouse-pointer".

4 Now click on Control in the blocks palette. All the blocks on the right of the palette will switch to orange.

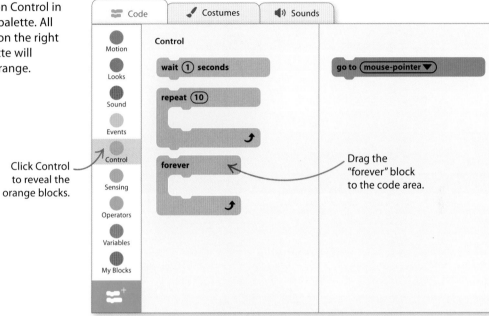

Click Control to reveal the orange blocks.

Drag the "forever" block to the code area.

5 Use the mouse to drag the "forever" block around the "go to mouse-pointer" block. It should click into place if you release it near the blue block. The "forever" block makes the blocks inside run over and over again.

This block is called a loop and repeats the blocks inside it.

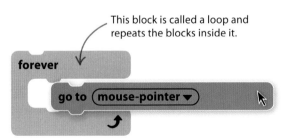

6 To complete your first bit of code, select Events in the blocks palette and then drag a "when green flag clicked" block to the top of your stack of blocks. This block makes the code run when someone clicks on the green flag symbol on the stage.

A block that goes at the top of the code is known as a header block.

7 Click on the green flag at the top of the stage. The cat will now go wherever the mouse-pointer goes. You can stop the chase with the red stop button. Congratulations on your first working Scratch code!

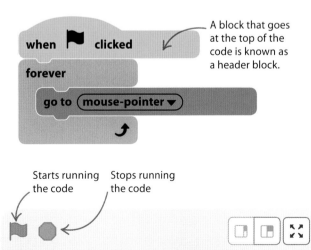

Starts running the code   Stops running the code

Multicolored cats

Scratch is packed full of ways to make art. The simple code changes here will send your cat straight to the art gallery.

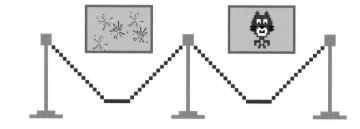

8 Click on Looks in the blocks palette and find the "change color effect by" block. Drag this into the loop in your code so it looks like this.

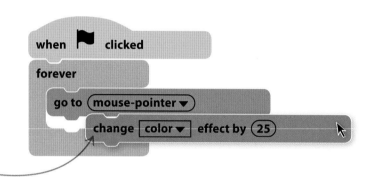

What do you think will happen when you run this new version of the code?

9. Click the green flag to run the new version of the project. The cat now changes color from moment to moment. Every time the loop repeats the "change color effect by" block, the sprite shifts in color a little.

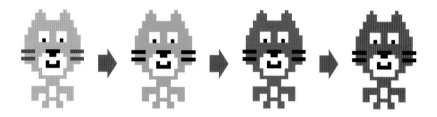

10 Now comes the moment to make some art. You need to add an extension. Click the Add Extension button at the bottom left and choose the Pen extension. Now you can click on Pen in the blocks palette, and you'll see a selection of green blocks. Drag a "stamp" block into the loop so your code looks like this.

Let's make some art!

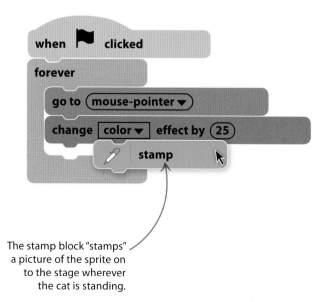

The stamp block "stamps" a picture of the sprite on to the stage wherever the cat is standing.

11 Next, run the project again by clicking the green flag. The cat will leave a trail of multicolored cats behind it. What an artistic cat!

Each cat in the trail is put there by the stamp block.

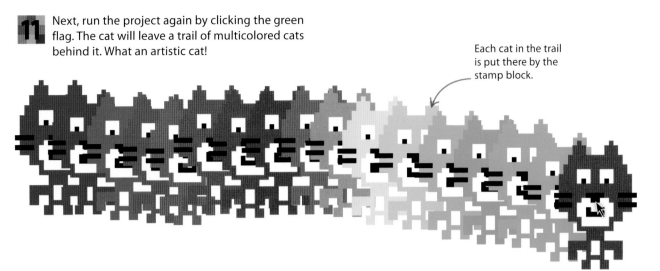

12 You'll find that the stage soon fills up with cats, but don't worry, because you can add code to wipe it clean at the press of a button. Choose Pen in the blocks palette and look for the "erase all" block. Drag it into the code area but keep it separate from the first code. Then click on Events and add a yellow "when space key pressed" block. Run the project and see what happens when you press the space bar.

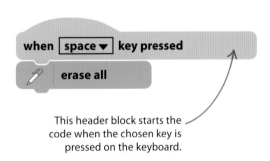

This header block starts the code when the chosen key is pressed on the keyboard.

EXPERT TIPS

Full screen

To see projects at their best, you can simply click the full-screen button just above the stage to hide the code and show only the results. There's a similar button to shrink the stage and reveal the code again from full-screen mode.

Click here to see your project fill the screen.

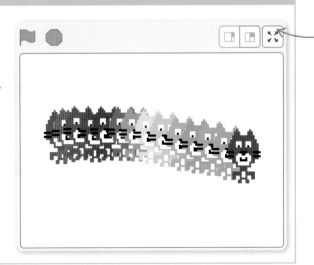

If you use the offline version of Scratch, don't forget to save your work from time to time.

Hacks and tweaks

There are lots of ways to change how the cat looks, and you can use them to create some startling visual effects. Below are a few tips, but feel free to try your own experiments.

▽ **Try this for size**
Add these two code blocks to the cat to make it bigger or smaller when you press the up or down arrow keys.

Click on the triangle to choose the correct key from a drop-down list.

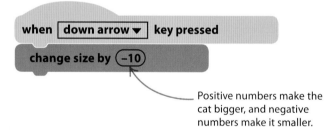

Positive numbers make the cat bigger, and negative numbers make it smaller.

Crazy cat

Try growing your cat until it fills the stage. Press the space bar to clear all the other cats, leave the computer mouse alone, and hold down the down arrow. A succession of ever-smaller cats will appear inside each other, creating a multicolored, cat-shaped tunnel!

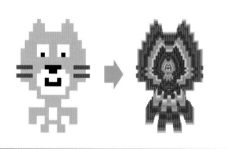

▽ **Smooth changes**
Don't be afraid to experiment with the numbers and settings in Scratch commands. You don't have to change the cat's color effect by 25 each time. The lower the number, the more slowly the color will change, like in this rainbow.

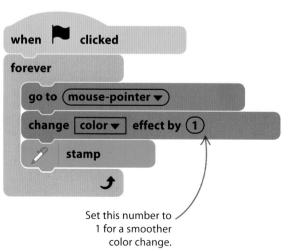

Set this number to 1 for a smoother color change.

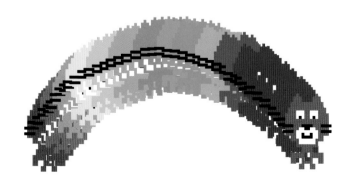

▽ Special effects

There are lots of other effects to try besides simple color changes. Try adding another "change" block to the main code. Click the drop-down menu and try the other effects to see what they do.

▽ Cleaning up

Things can get messy with effects, so add a "clear graphic effects" block to the code below. This runs when you press the space bar to clear the stage.

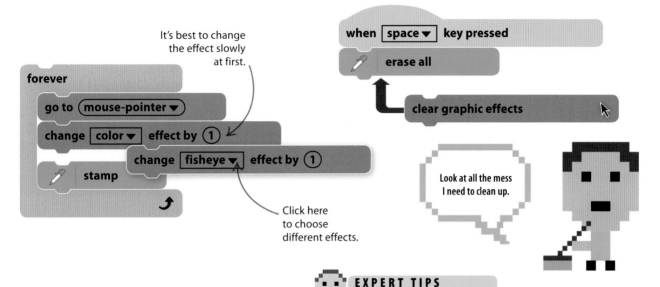

It's best to change the effect slowly at first.

Click here to choose different effects.

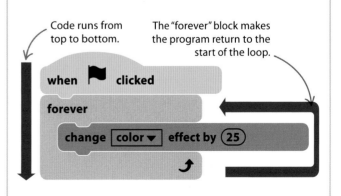

clear graphic effects

Look at all the mess I need to clean up.

▽ At your fingertips

To give yourself more control over effects while painting with the cat, you can trigger code blocks with any keys you choose. You could create a whole keyboard full of weird cat changes, including the ghost effect shown here.

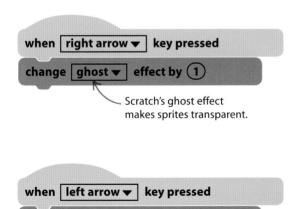

Scratch's ghost effect makes sprites transparent.

EXPERT TIPS

Loops

Almost all computer programs contain loops. These are useful because they let a program go back and repeat a set of instructions, which keeps code blocks simple and short. The "forever" block creates a loop that goes on forever, but other types of loops can repeat an action a fixed number of times. You'll meet all sorts of clever loops in projects later in the book.

Code runs from top to bottom.

The "forever" block makes the program return to the start of the loop.

when ⚑ clicked

forever

change color ▼ effect by 25

Dino Dance Party

Brush off your dancing shoes and join the dinosaur's dance party! Who will you invite? There will be music, a light show, and dance moves galore. Dance routines are just like computer programs—you just follow the steps in order.

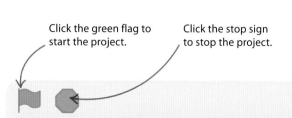

Click the green flag to start the project.

Click the stop sign to stop the project.

How it works

Each sprite has one or more blocks of code that program its dance moves. Some simply turn from side to side, but others glide across the dance floor or perform more varied moves. You can add as many dancers as you like.

◁ **Dinosaur**
After you've created a dancing dinosaur, you can duplicate this sprite to make a group of dinosaurs dancing in rhythm.

The "Spotlight" backdrop sets the scene for the dance party.

◁ **Ballerina**
To add a touch of class, the ballerina will perform a more complicated dance routine.

The disco lights change color several times a second.

Click this icon to escape the full-screen mode.

By switching between different poses, the sprites appear to dance.

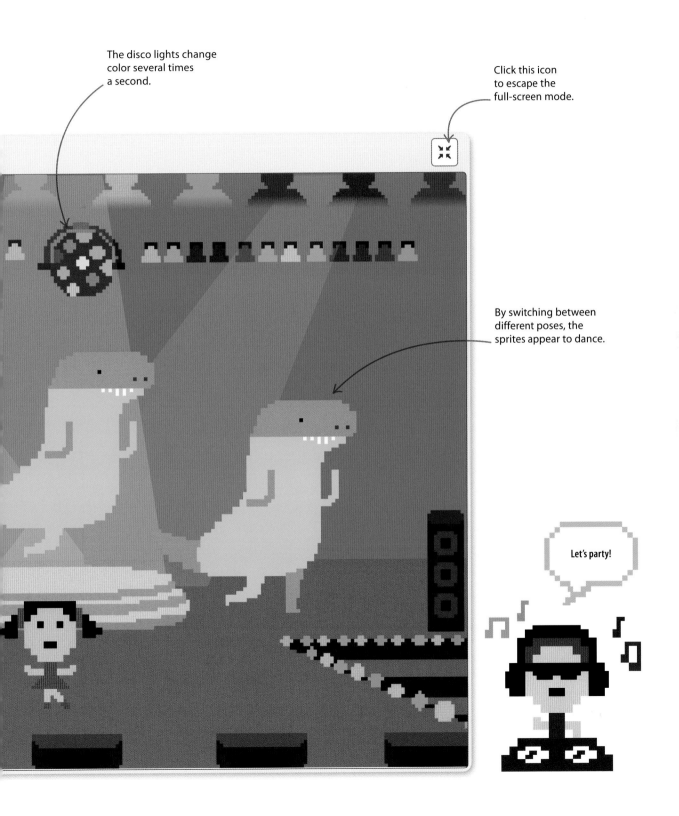

Let's party!

Dancing dinosaur

Scratch has lots of ready-made sprites for your project in the sprites library. Many of the sprites have several "costumes," each showing the sprite in a different pose. If you make a sprite switch costumes quickly, it looks like it's moving.

1 First, start a fresh Scratch project. From the main Scratch website, click on Create at the top. If a Scratch project is already open, click on the File menu above the stage and select "New".

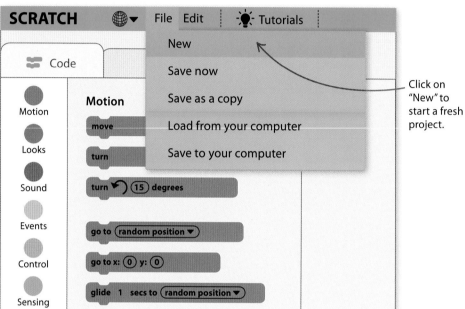

Click on "New" to start a fresh project.

2 New projects always start with the cat sprite, but you don't need it this time. To delete it, right-click on the cat (or control/shift-click on a one-button mouse) and select "delete". The cat will disappear.

3 To load a new sprite, click on the small sprite symbol 🐱 in the sprites list just below the stage. A window with a huge selection of sprites will open. Choose Dinosaur4. It will now appear on the stage and in the sprites list.

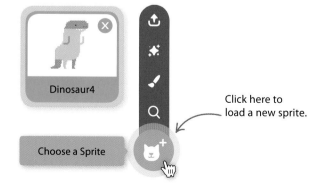

Click here to load a new sprite.

4 Make this simple code for Dinosaur4. Look carefully, and you'll see the code runs when the space bar is pressed—not when the green flag is clicked.

You can find yellow blocks by clicking on Events in the blocks palette.

Click on Looks to find purple blocks.

when space ▼ key pressed

next costume

5 Look at the dinosaur on the stage and press the space bar. Every time you press it, the dinosaur will change its pose. It's still the Dinosaur4 sprite, but the way it looks keeps changing. Each different pose is called a costume and can be used to make a sprite appear to do different things.

Each pose is a different costume belonging to the dinosaur sprite.

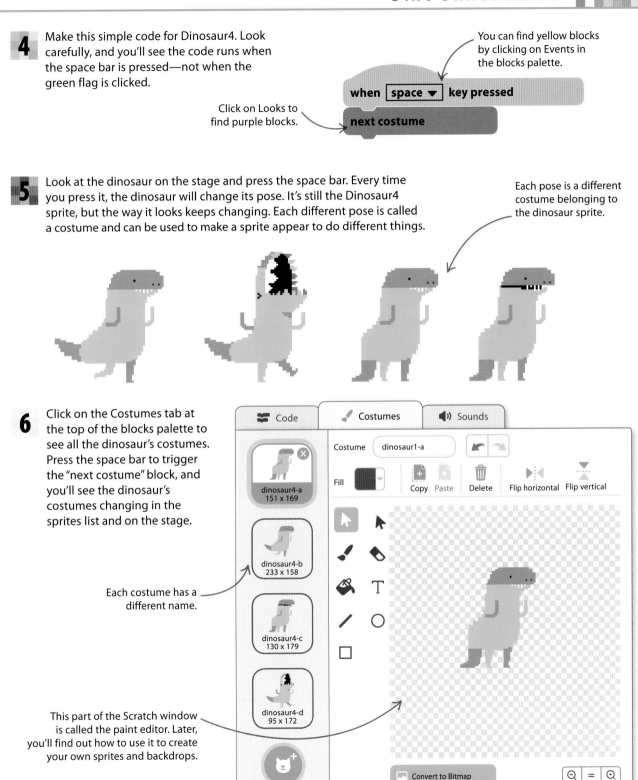

6 Click on the Costumes tab at the top of the blocks palette to see all the dinosaur's costumes. Press the space bar to trigger the "next costume" block, and you'll see the dinosaur's costumes changing in the sprites list and on the stage.

Each costume has a different name.

This part of the Scratch window is called the paint editor. Later, you'll find out how to use it to create your own sprites and backdrops.

Code   Costumes   Sounds

Costume   dinosaur1-a

Fill   Copy   Paste   Delete   Flip horizontal   Flip vertical

dinosaur4-a
151 x 169

dinosaur4-b
233 x 158

dinosaur4-c
130 x 179

dinosaur4-d
95 x 172

Convert to Bitmap

Dance steps

By using loops, you can make the dinosaur change its costume repeatedly, making it appear to move. Changing pictures quickly to give the illusion of movement is called animation.

7 Click on the Code tab at the top of the Scratch window to go back to the dinosaur's code blocks and add this code. Before you try it, read through the code and see wheher you can figure out what it does.

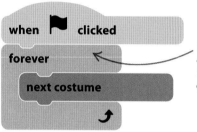

Remember, blocks are color coded. The "forever" loop is in the orange Control blocks section.

8 Click the green flag above the stage to run the code. You'll see the dinosaur move wildly as it loops through all its costumes at high speed. To make a neater dance, the next step will limit the number of costumes to just two.

dinosaur4-c   dinosaur4-d

9 Remove the "next costume" block from the loop and replace it with the blocks shown here. The new code switches between two costumes and slows everything down with some "wait" blocks. Run the project again by clicking the green flag—the dinosaur should now dance more sensibly.

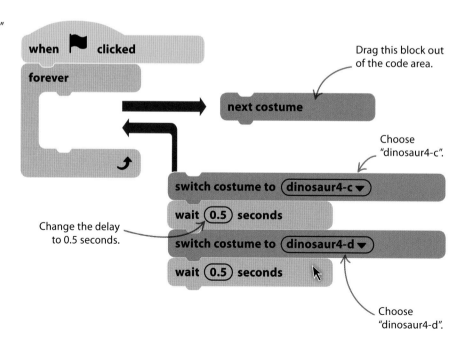

Drag this block out of the code area.

Choose "dinosaur4-c".

Change the delay to 0.5 seconds.

Choose "dinosaur4-d".

10 To add more dancing dinosaurs to the party, you can simply copy the first dinosaur. Right-click on the dinosaur in the sprites list and choose "duplicate" from the drop-down menu. A new dinosaur will appear in the sprites list.

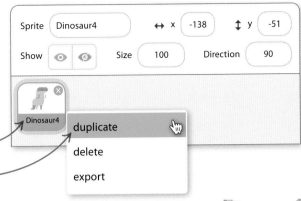

Right-click (or shift/ctrl-click) on the dinosaur.

Choose "duplicate" to make a copy of the sprite and its code.

11 Make another copy so that there are three dinosaurs in total. Click on the dinosaurs on the stage and drag each one to a good spot. Run the project. Since they all have the same code, they'll all do the same dance at the same time.

Setting the scene

The dinosaurs are dancing, but the room's a bit boring. Follow the next steps to add some decorations and music. You'll need to make some changes to the stage. Although it isn't a sprite, it can still have its own code.

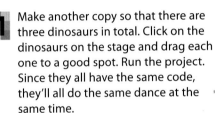

12 First, a change of scenery. The picture on the stage is called a backdrop, and you can load new ones. Look at the bottom right of the screen and click on the backdrop symbol 🖼 to the right of the sprites list.

Click this symbol to add a backdrop.

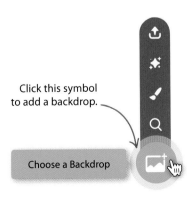

Choose a Backdrop

13 Search for "Spotlight" in the backdrops library and select it. This backdrop will now appear behind the dancers.

The "Spotlight" backdrop sets the mood of the party.

14 Now, click on the Code tab at the top of the screen to add some code to the stage. Each sprite can have its own code, and so can the stage.

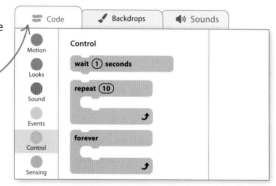

Click here to show the code area.

15 Add this code to make the disco lights flash. Then click the green flag to run the project—it should look like a real disco. You can experiment with the time in the "wait" block to make the lights flash faster or slower if you want.

Adjust the number here to change how fast the lights flash.

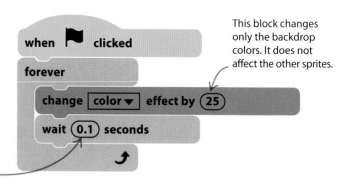

This block changes only the backdrop colors. It does not affect the other sprites.

16 Now it's time to add some music. Click on the Sounds tab, which is next to the Backdrops tab at the top. Then click on the speaker symbol ◄» to open Scratch's sound library. Select "Dance Around", and it will load into the stage's list of sound clips.

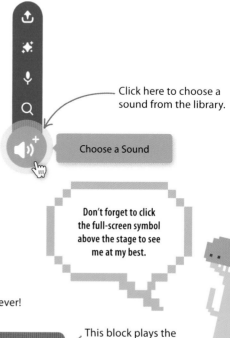

Click here to choose a sound from the library.

17 Click on the Code tab again and add this new code to play the music in a loop. Click the green flag to run the project again. The music should play. You now have a real party on your hands!

The music repeats forever!

Don't forget to click the full-screen symbol above the stage to see me at my best.

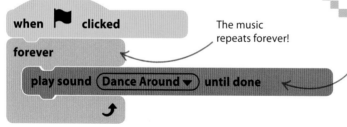

This block plays the whole tune before the code goes back to the start.

Get a move on!

The dinosaurs are throwing some wicked shapes, but they're not moving around the dance floor much. You can fix that with some new code blocks that use Scratch's "move" block.

18 First, click on Dinosaur2 in the sprites list to show its code in the code area.

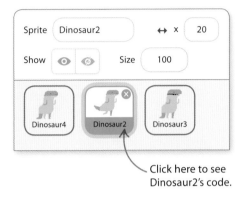

Click here to see Dinosaur2's code.

19 Next, add this extra code. To find the dark blue blocks, click Motion at the top of the blocks palette. What do you think the new code does?

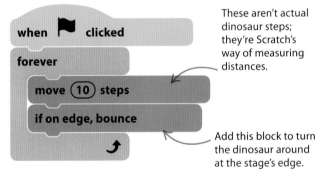

These aren't actual dinosaur steps; they're Scratch's way of measuring distances.

Add this block to turn the dinosaur around at the stage's edge.

20 Now, click the green flag, and both of Dinosaur2's code blocks will run at the same time. The sprite will move all the way across the stage and then turn around and dance back. But you'll notice that it dances back upside down!

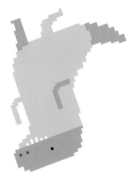

21 To prevent the blood from rushing to the dinosaur's tiny brain, add the "set rotation style" block like this. You now have the power to choose whether the dinosaur dances on its head or not.

Select "left-right" in the drop-down menu to keep the dinosaur upright.

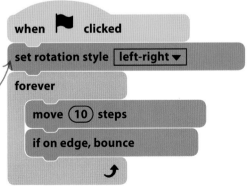

Keyboard control

Ever dreamed of taking control of your very own dinosaur?
The next bit of code will give you keyboard control of
Dinosaur3's movements; you'll be able to move the dinosaur
across the stage with the right and left arrow keys.

22 Click on Dinosaur3 in the sprites list so you can edit its code.

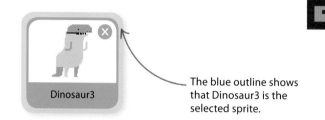

Dinosaur3

The blue outline shows that Dinosaur3 is the selected sprite.

23 Add this code to the code area. It's quite complicated, so make sure you get everything in the right place. The "if then" block is in the orange Control blocks section. It's a special block that chooses whether or not to run the blocks inside it by asking a question. Take care to ensure that both "if then" blocks are inside the "forever" loop and not inside each other.

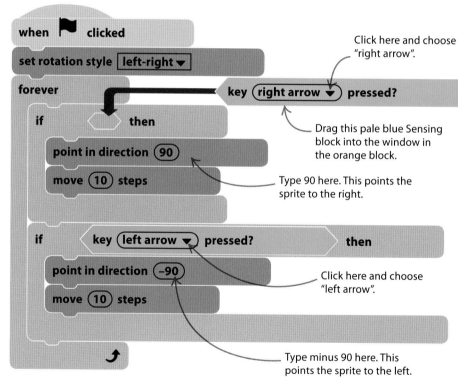

when 🏳 clicked

set rotation style [left-right ▼]

forever

if ⬡ then
    point in direction (90)
    move (10) steps

if ⟨ key (left arrow ▼) pressed? ⟩ then
    point in direction (–90)
    move (10) steps

Click here and choose "right arrow".

key (right arrow ▼) pressed?

Drag this pale blue Sensing block into the window in the orange block.

Type 90 here. This points the sprite to the right.

Click here and choose "left arrow".

Type minus 90 here. This points the sprite to the left.

24 Before you run the code, read through it carefully and see whether you can understand how it works. If the right arrow key is pressed, blocks that make the sprite point right and move are run. If the left arrow key is pressed, blocks that make the sprite point left and move are run. If neither is pressed, no blocks are run, and the dinosaur stays put.

Making choices

You make choices all the time. If you're hungry, you decide to eat; if not, you don't. Computer programs can also make choices between different options. One way to make them do this is to use an "if then" instruction, which is used in lots of programming languages. In Scratch, the "if then" block includes a statement or a question and runs the code inside the block only if the statement is true (or the answer is yes).

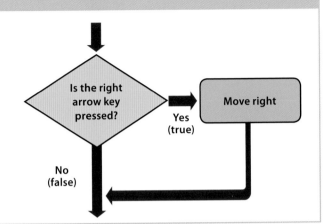

Add a ballerina

The dinosaurs are dancing, but it's not much of a party without some friends. A ballerina is going to join the fun and will do a routine. Her code will show you how to create more complicated dance routines.

25 Click on the sprite symbol 🐱 in the sprites list and load the ballerina. Then use your mouse to drag the sprite to a good spot on the stage. To give the ballerina some code, make sure she's selected in the sprites list—the selected sprite has a blue outline.

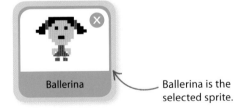

Ballerina is the selected sprite.

26 You can see all the costumes of a sprite by clicking on the Costumes tab when the sprite is selected. The ballerina has four costumes, and switching between them will make her dance a beautiful ballet.

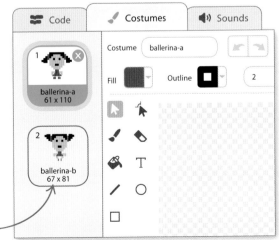

Each costume has a unique name.

27 Using the names of the different costumes, you can design a dance routine for the ballerina, like the one shown here. Each step in the dance will become an instruction block in the code.

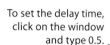 Costume ballerina-a then ballerina-d, repeated three times.

28 Build this code to create the ballerina's first dance. There's no "forever" loop—instead, the code uses a "repeat" loop that runs a fixed number of times before moving on to the next block. Run the project to see her perform the dance routine.

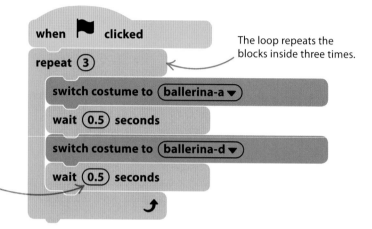

The loop repeats the blocks inside three times.

To set the delay time, click on the window and type 0.5.

```
when [flag] clicked
repeat (3)
    switch costume to (ballerina-a ▾)
    wait (0.5) seconds
    switch costume to (ballerina-d ▾)
    wait (0.5) seconds
```

. . . LINGO

Algorithms

An algorithm is a series of simple, step-by-step instructions that together carry out a particular task. In this project, you converted the ballerina's dance routine (an algorithm) into a program. Every computer program has an algorithm at its heart. Programming is translating the steps of the algorithm into a computer programming language that the computer understands.

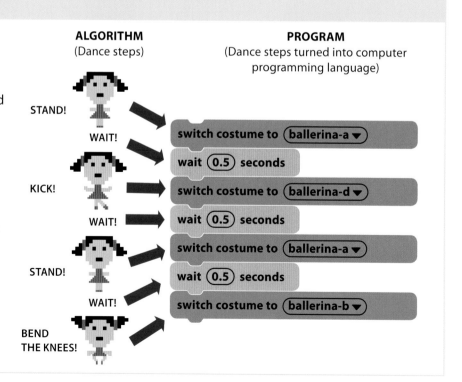

ALGORITHM
(Dance steps)

STAND!
WAIT!
KICK!
WAIT!
STAND!
WAIT!
BEND THE KNEES!

PROGRAM
(Dance steps turned into computer programming language)

switch costume to (ballerina-a ▾)
wait (0.5) seconds
switch costume to (ballerina-d ▾)
wait (0.5) seconds
switch costume to (ballerina-a ▾)
wait (0.5) seconds
switch costume to (ballerina-b ▾)

29 Now for the second part of the ballerina's routine. After flexing her leg three times, she'll dip twice.

Costume ballerina-a then ballerina-b, repeated twice.

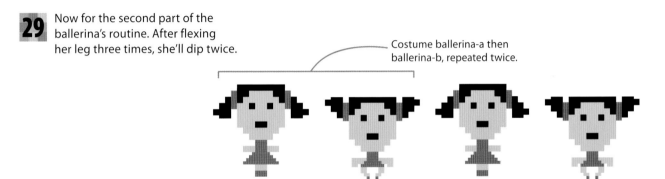

30 Add the blocks shown here to the bottom of the ballerina's code, after the first "repeat" block.

31 Next, click the green flag, and you'll see the ballerina do her full routine. But she'll do the routine only once. To make the dance go on, you can wrap the whole body of the code in a "forever" loop. Loops inside loops!

Drag the "forever" loop to the top of the existing code, and the jaws will expand to fit.

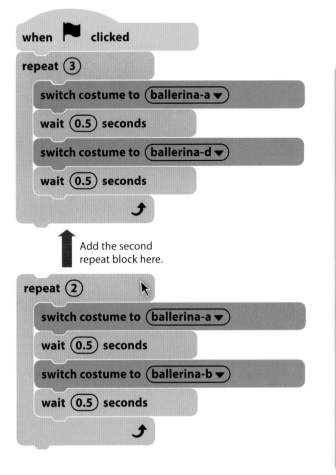

Add the second repeat block here.

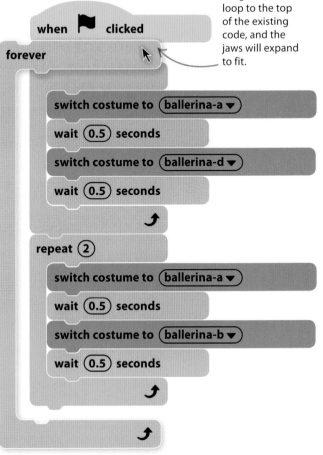

Repeat loops and forever loops

Look at the bottom of the two types of loops you've used so far. Which one can have blocks attached to it? You might notice that the "repeat" block has a small lug on the bottom, but the "forever" block doesn't. There's no lug on a "forever" loop because it goes on forever, so there's no point adding blocks after it. A "repeat" block, however, runs a fixed number of times, and the code then continues.

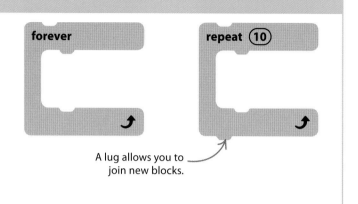

A lug allows you to join new blocks.

Hacks and tweaks

You can add as many dancers as you like to this project. There are lots of sprites in Scratch that have several costumes, and even those with only a single costume can be instructed to dance by flipping left to right or by jumping in the air.

▽ **Turn around**
You can make any character face the other way by using a "turn 180 degrees" block. Just add this block before the end of the "forever" loop to make your sprite's dance switch direction each time.

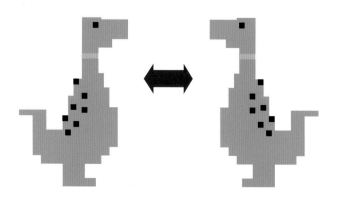

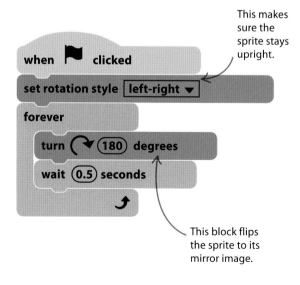

This makes sure the sprite stays upright.

```
when 🏳 clicked
set rotation style  left-right ▼
forever
    turn ↻ 180 degrees
    wait 0.5 seconds
```

This block flips the sprite to its mirror image.

▷ Dance off!

Look in the library for other dancing sprites. They have lots of costumes showing different dance postures. Start off with some simple code like this one that shows all the costumes in order. Then choose the costumes that work best together and switch between them. Add loops to extend the dance or add sensing blocks to give you keyboard control.

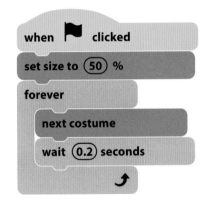

▽ Might as well jump!

Add another ballerina, and make her jump in the air with this code. The change of costume makes it seem like the ballerina is really jumping. Experiment with the timing to make the dance match the music.

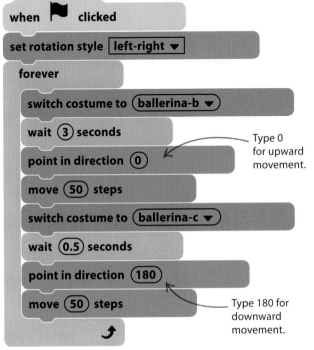

Type 0 for upward movement.

Type 180 for downward movement.

▪ ▪ ▪ TRY THIS

Shout!

Add this short bit of code to every one of your sprites. When you press the x key, all the sprites will shout "Party!"

PARTY!

Animal Race

Have you ever wondered which is faster—a dog or a bat? Now you can find out when you play this fun fast-finger, button-pressing, two-player animal race game.

How it works

The aim of this two-player game is simply to race across the screen and reach the balloons before the other player. Fast-finger action is all you need to win. The faster you tap the keyboard's "z" or "m" key, the faster your sprite moves from left to right.

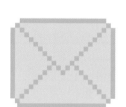

◁ **Sending messages**
This project shows you how to use Scratch's message feature to make one sprite pass information to other sprites, such as when the cat sprite tells the dog and bat to start racing.

Count

◁ **Variables**
The cat's code stores information in something programmers call a variable. In this project, you'll use a variable to store the numbers for the cat's count at the start of the race.

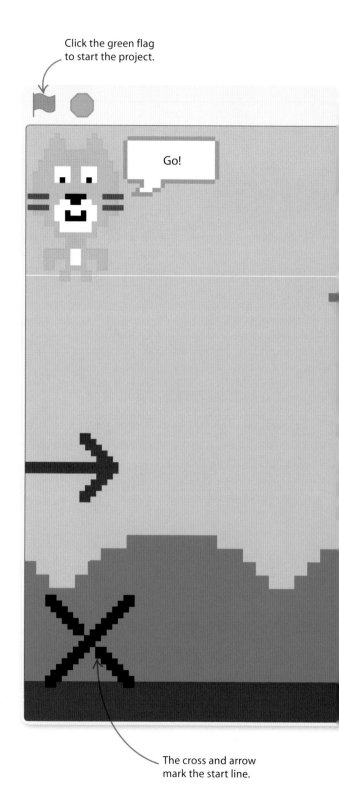

Click the green flag to start the project.

Go!

The cross and arrow mark the start line.

The bat flaps its wings every time you press the "z" key.

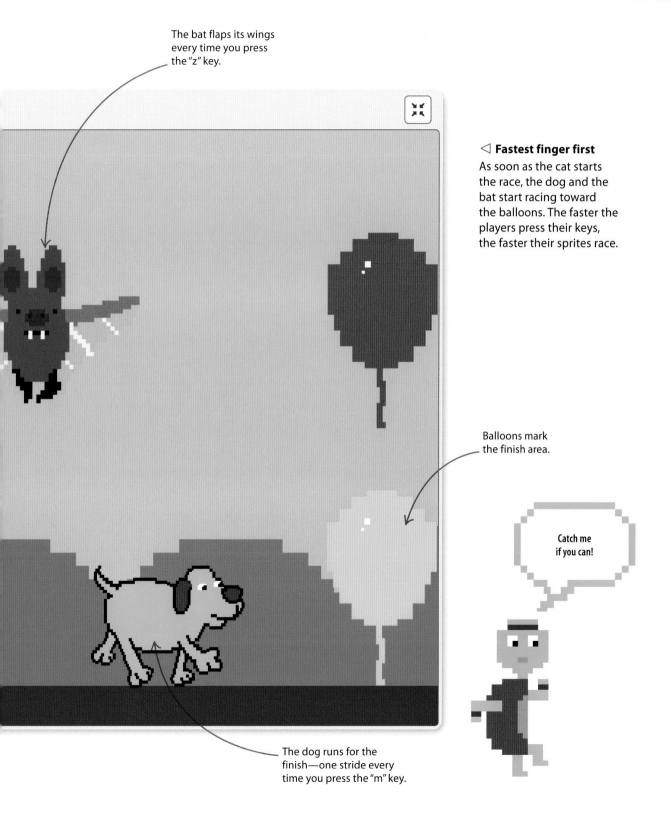

◁ **Fastest finger first**
As soon as the cat starts the race, the dog and the bat start racing toward the balloons. The faster the players press their keys, the faster their sprites race.

Balloons mark the finish area.

Catch me if you can!

The dog runs for the finish—one stride every time you press the "m" key.

Starter cat

The cat starts the race with "1 … 2 … 3 … Go!" so you need to teach him how to count. Computer programs use variables to store information that can change, such as players' names or their score in a game. The cat will use a variable named "Count" to keep track of what number he's gotten up to.

1 Start a new project. To create a new variable, select the orange Variables block in the blocks palette, and click on the "Make a Variable" button.

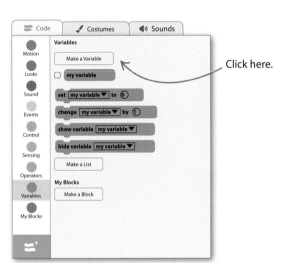

Click here.

2 A small window will pop up asking you to give the new variable a name. Type "Count", leave everything else alone, and click the "OK" button.

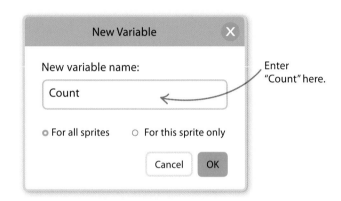

Enter "Count" here.

3 You'll now see some orange blocks for the new variable in the blocks palette. Uncheck the variable's check box so that it doesn't appear on the stage.

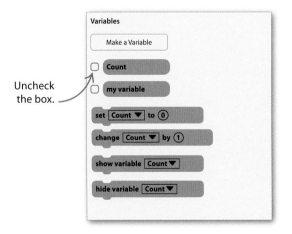

Uncheck the box.

4 Give this code to the cat. It starts by setting the value of "Count" to 0. Next, inside a loop, it adds 1 to the value of "Count" and makes the cat say the new value for one second. The loop runs three times, and then the cat says "Go!" to start the race.

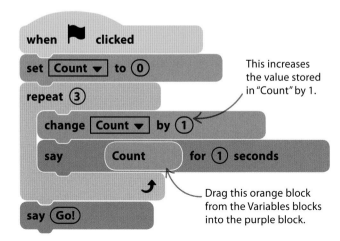

This increases the value stored in "Count" by 1.

Drag this orange block from the Variables blocks into the purple block.

5 Click the green flag to run the code. The orange "Count" block in the window of the "say" block makes the cat say the variable's value each time. You can change how high the cat counts by changing the number in the "repeat" loop's window.

Variables

Think of a variable as a box for storing information, with a label to remember what's inside. When you create a variable, give it a sensible name, such as "High Score" or "Player Name." You can put all sorts of data into variables, including numbers and words, and the data can change while the program is running.

High Score

Setting up the racers

The cat is ready to start the race. The next steps are to decorate the stage for the race and then to add the bat and the dog sprites, along with other sprites to mark the start and end of the racetrack.

6 Add a backdrop. Click on the backdrop symbol ▦ to the right of the sprites list and add the "Blue Sky" backdrop.

Click here to open the backdrop library.

Choose a Backdrop

7 It's time to add some sprites for the racers, starting with the dog. Click the sprite symbol 🐱 in the sprites list. Find Dog2 in the library and add it to your project.

Dog2 will now appear in the sprites list.

8 Make sure Dog2 is selected in the sprites list. Click on the Costumes tab at the top of the Scratch window, and you'll see it has three costumes. The first two show the dog running, but you don't need the third one so delete it.

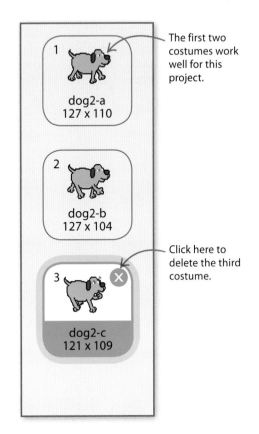

The first two costumes work well for this project.

dog2-a
127 x 110

dog2-b
127 x 104

Click here to delete the third costume.

dog2-c
121 x 109

9 To tell the dog where to start the race, add another new sprite, Button5, which is a black cross. Drag it to the bottom left of the stage.

The black cross tells the dog where to start the race.

10 Every sprite you load should have a meaningful name. This makes code easier to understand. To rename Button5, click on the sprite and name it "Dog Start".

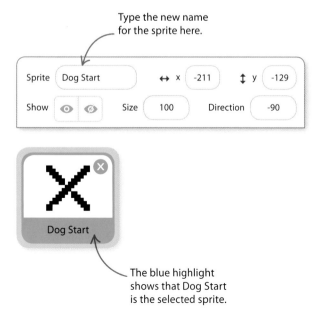

Type the new name for the sprite here.

Sprite	Dog Start	↔ x	-211	↕ y	-129
Show	👁 👁	Size	100	Direction	-90

The blue highlight shows that Dog Start is the selected sprite.

11 Select Dog2 again. Then click the Code tab at the top of the Scratch window, and add this code to make the dog start in the correct place. Run the project to see it in action.

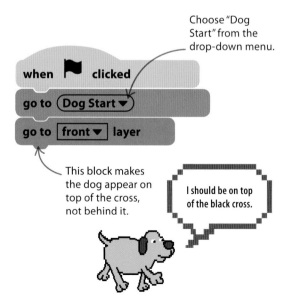

Choose "Dog Start" from the drop-down menu.

when 🏳 clicked
go to Dog Start ▼
go to front ▼ layer

This block makes the dog appear on top of the cross, not behind it.

I should be on top of the black cross.

12 Now add a new sprite for the dog's finish line. Choose Balloon1, but rename it "Dog Finish". To change the balloon's color, click on the Costumes tab and choose the yellow costume. On the stage, drag the sprite to the finish point of the dog's race.

Remember to choose the yellow balloon for the dog.

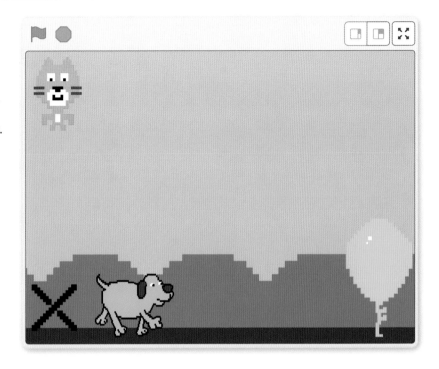

13 The dog needs someone to race against. Click the sprite symbol  in the sprites list again and add Bat to the project. Click the Costumes tab, and you'll see two costumes perfect for flapping.

14 Now add the Arrow1 sprite, but rename it "Bat Start" and drag it just above the cross. Then add another balloon, rename it "Bat Finish", and place it at the bat's finish line on the right.

The bat has to touch the balloon to finish the race.

15 Select the bat sprite in the sprites list and give it this code. Run the project and watch the competitors line up at the start.

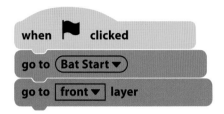

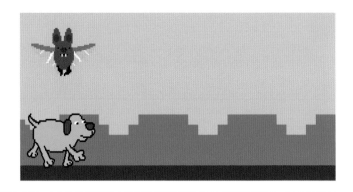

The race

The bat and the dog both need code to make them race. The cat will trigger these code blocks by sending a message when it says "Go!" at the start of the race. Both contestants will receive the message at exactly the same time.

16 Select the cat sprite in the sprites list and add a "broadcast" block to the bottom of its code. This block sends out a message to every other sprite.

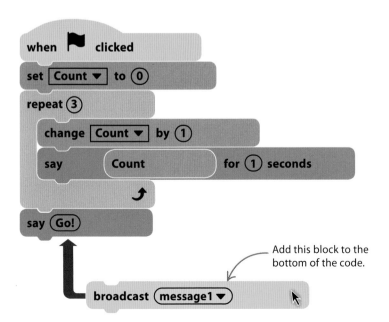

Add this block to the bottom of the code.

17 Click on the triangle in the "broadcast" block and choose "New message" from the drop-down menu. Type "Start Race" as the name of the new message and click "OK".

Open the drop-down menu by clicking here.

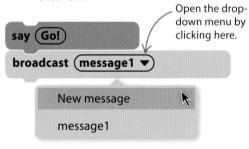

18 Now the cat sends out the "Start Race" message at the start of the race. Each racer needs some code to make it react, so select the dog first and add this code. See how the two "wait until" blocks together make the player press the "m" key and then release it again and again to move his character; just keeping your finger on the "m" key won't work.

Make sure the message in here is "Start Race".

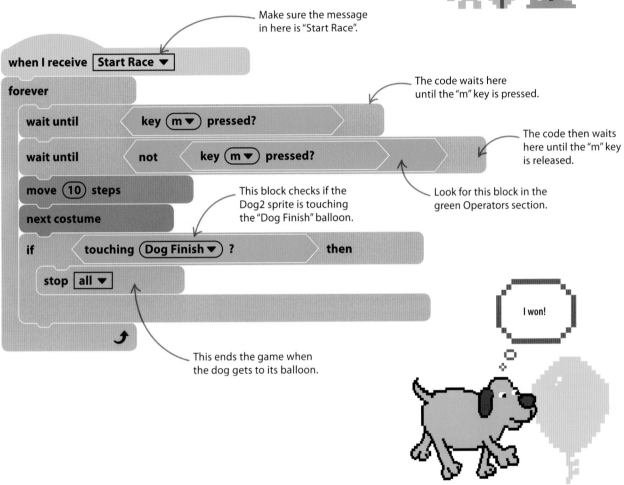

```
when I receive  Start Race ▼
forever
    wait until          key (m ▼) pressed?
    wait until      not      key (m ▼) pressed?
    move (10) steps
    next costume
    if      touching (Dog Finish ▼) ?      then
        stop  all ▼
```

The code waits here until the "m" key is pressed.

The code then waits here until the "m" key is released.

This block checks if the Dog2 sprite is touching the "Dog Finish" balloon.

Look for this block in the green Operators section.

This ends the game when the dog gets to its balloon.

I won!

⋅ ⋅ ⋅ LINGO

Boolean operator: NOT

The "not" block reverses the answer to the question block inside it. This block is very useful for testing if something *isn't* happening. There are three green Operators blocks that can change

answers to yes/no questions (or true/false statements) in useful ways: "not," "or," and "and." Programmers call these "Boolean operators," and you'll use all of them in this book.

19 Run the project. Once the cat says "Go!" you should find that the dog runs forward a step each time you press and release the "m" key. When it reaches its balloon, the dog should stop responding. If anything isn't working, carefully check your code against the version in the book.

20 Next, add this similar code to the bat sprite. The only differences are that the key selected now is the "z" key, and the bat must touch its own finish sprite.

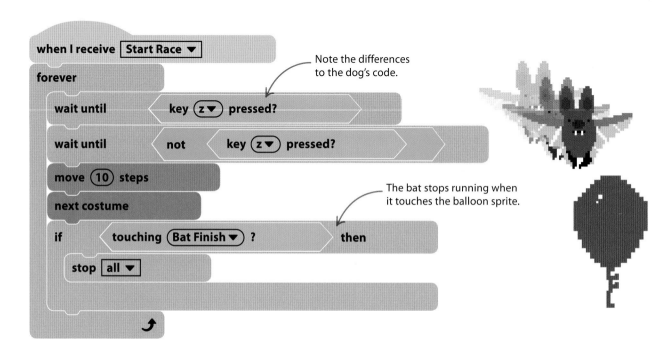

when I receive Start Race ▼

forever

> wait until ⟨ key (z ▼) pressed? ⟩

> wait until ⟨ not ⟨ key (z ▼) pressed? ⟩ ⟩

> move (10) steps

> next costume

> if ⟨ touching (Bat Finish ▼) ? ⟩ then

>> stop all ▼

Note the differences to the dog's code.

The bat stops running when it touches the balloon sprite.

21 Now try to race the sprites. You might find that one sprite wins more easily because a wing or a nose sticks out. You can drag the start and finish sprites around a little to even things up.

Drag the cat to the corner, out of the way of the racers.

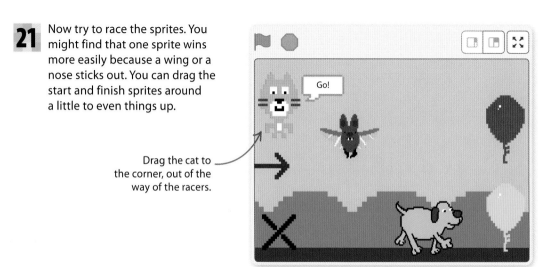

Go!

Hacks and tweaks

The race game is very simple, but you can easily add features to make it more interesting. Here are some suggestions to get you started. It's worth making a copy of your project before you start to change things—then you won't be afraid to experiment.

▷ **Sounds**
Add a sound effect to mark the start of the race by adding a "start sound" block to the cat's code. The cat has the "Meow" sound preloaded, but you can load other sounds from the sound library by clicking the Sounds tab and then the speaker symbol ◀》.

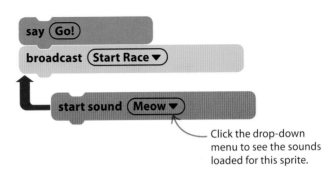

Click the drop-down menu to see the sounds loaded for this sprite.

Change 0 to 4.

Place a minus sign in front of 1.

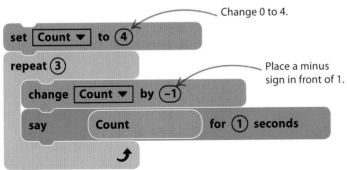

◁ **Countdown**
Try changing the middle part of the cat's code to look like this. Can you figure out what will happen now?

I'm the fastest!

◁ **Extra competitors**
Why not add more animals to the race? Find some sprites in the sprites library with costumes you can animate, like the parrot or Butterfly 1. Add start and end sprites for each one of them and adapt the racing code to use different keys. If you need to adjust a sprite's size, just add a "set size to" block.

▽ **Challenging controls**

You can make the game harder for the players by making them press two keys alternately instead of one key repeatedly. You just need to change the code to wait for a second key to be pressed and released after the first one. This shows how to change the dog's code. For the bat, make the same change but use "x" for the second key instead of "n."

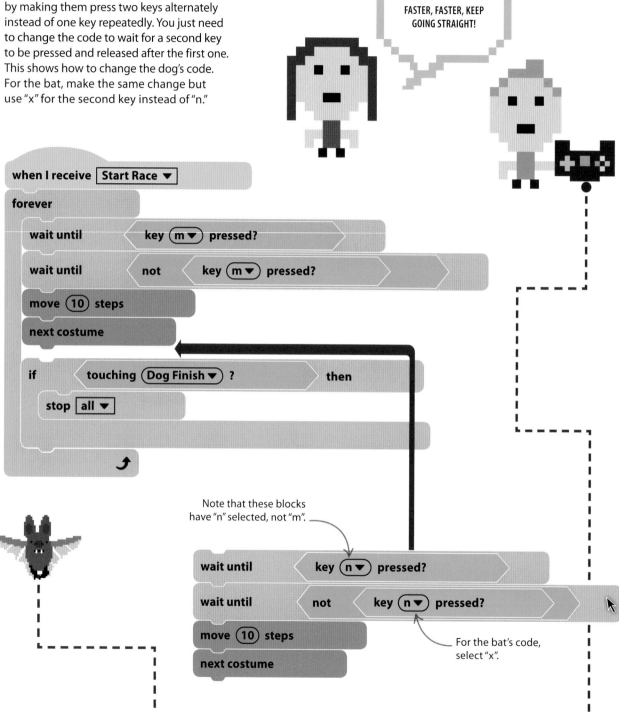

FASTER, FASTER, KEEP GOING STRAIGHT!

when I receive | Start Race ▼

forever

wait until | key (m ▼) pressed?

wait until | not | key (m ▼) pressed?

move (10) steps

next costume

if | touching (Dog Finish ▼) ? | then

stop | all ▼

Note that these blocks have "n" selected, not "m".

wait until | key (n ▼) pressed?

wait until | not | key (n ▼) pressed?

move (10) steps

next costume

For the bat's code, select "x".

Race positions

It might not always be easy to tell who's won if the finish is close. To fix this, you can make the animals show their finishing position when the game ends.

1 Choose Variables in the blocks palette and then click the "Make a Variable" button to create a new variable. Call it "Position".

New Variable	✕

New variable name:

Position

○ For all sprites   ○ For this sprite only

Cancel   OK

2 Next, add a "set Position to" block to the bottom of the cat's code and change the number to 1.

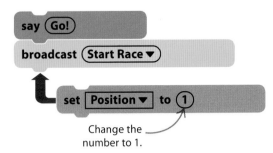

say Go!

broadcast Start Race ▼

set Position ▼ to 1

Change the number to 1.

3 Now change the end of the dog's code so it looks like this. You need to add two new blocks and choose a new menu option in the "stop" block. Do the same for the bat.

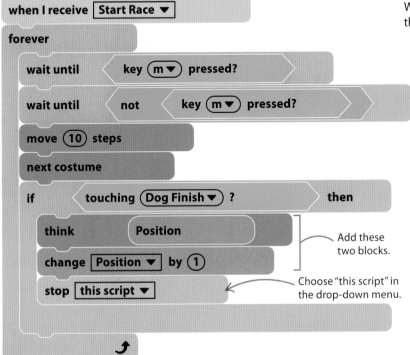

when I receive Start Race ▼

forever

wait until key m ▼ pressed?

wait until not key m ▼ pressed?

move 10 steps

next costume

if touching Dog Finish ▼ ? then

think Position

change Position ▼ by 1

stop this script ▼

Add these two blocks.

Choose "this script" in the drop-down menu.

4 Try it out. The cat's code sets "Position" to 1. The first sprite to reach the finish runs the "think Position" block, which makes a thought bubble containing the number 1 appear. Their code then adds 1 to the value of "Position", making it 2. When the second sprite finishes and thinks of "Position", it displays 2.

Ask Gobo

Do you have a tricky decision to make or want to predict the future? Let Gobo help you in this fortune-telling project. Here you'll learn about random numbers, variables, and how computer programs make choices.

The green flag starts the project.

The red button stops the project.

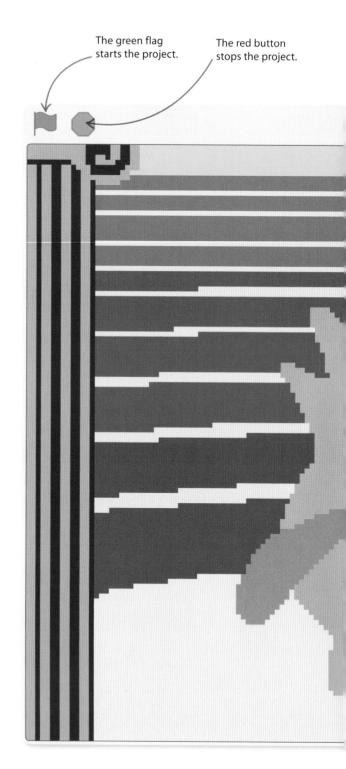

How it works

Gobo invites you to ask a question and then answers with either "Yes" or "No." You can ask anything you like, from "Am I going to be a billionaire?" to "Should I play a computer game instead of doing my homework?" Gobo pauses to look as if it's thinking, but its answers are actually pure chance.

◁ **Gobo**
Friendly Gobo is the only sprite in this project. It has three costumes that you can use later to help bring it to life.

◁ **Take a chance**
Just as the roll of the die creates random numbers, Scratch can generate random numbers to make the program react in unpredictable ways.

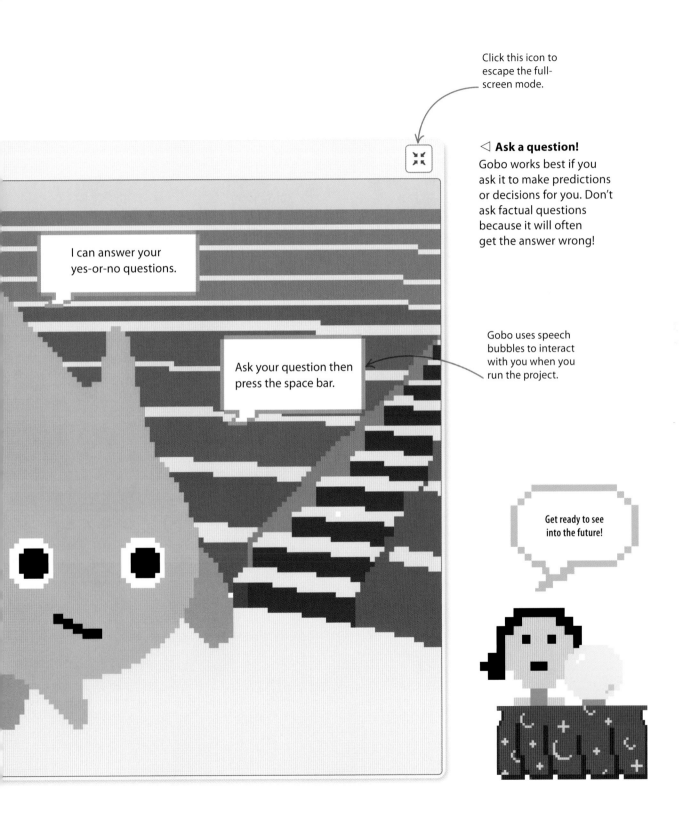

Click this icon to escape the full-screen mode.

◁ **Ask a question!**
Gobo works best if you ask it to make predictions or decisions for you. Don't ask factual questions because it will often get the answer wrong!

I can answer your yes-or-no questions.

Ask your question then press the space bar.

Gobo uses speech bubbles to interact with you when you run the project.

Get ready to see into the future!

Setting the scene

Starting a project usually involves picking sprites and backdrops. Follow these steps to add the Gobo sprite to the project and to load a suitable backdrop to create a grand setting for Gobo's answers.

1 Start a new project. Then get rid of the cat sprite by pressing the delete button at the top right of its icon in the sprites list.

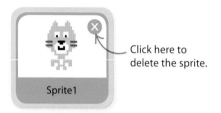

Click here to delete the sprite.

Sprite1

2 To load the Gobo sprite, click on the sprite symbol 🐱 in the sprites list and search for Gobo. Click on its icon. Gobo will now appear in the sprites list.

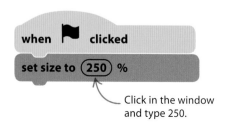

Gobo

3 Gobo's a bit small, so add this code to make it bigger. Run the project and see it grow.

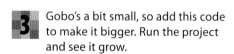

when 🚩 clicked

set size to (250) %

Click in the window and type 250.

4 Gobo's answers should be spoken in a serious setting. Click on the backdrop symbol 🖼 in the lower-right corner of the Scratch window and load the "Greek Theater" backdrop. Now drag Gobo to the center with your mouse.

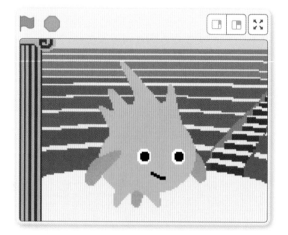

5 Now add these extra blocks to Gobo's code to make it speak when the project starts. Run the new code, and you'll see that Gobo pauses until you press the space bar. It won't answer yet.

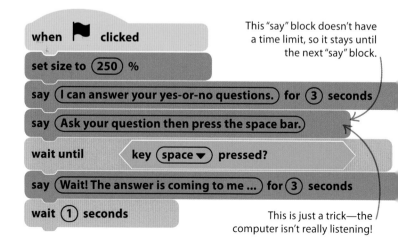

when 🚩 clicked

set size to (250) %

say (I can answer your yes-or-no questions.) for (3) seconds

say (Ask your question then press the space bar.)

wait until < key (space ▼) pressed? >

say (Wait! The answer is coming to me ...) for (3) seconds

wait (1) seconds

This "say" block doesn't have a time limit, so it stays until the next "say" block.

This is just a trick—the computer isn't really listening!

Making random choices

Computers are usually very predictable. Often, with the same code and inputs, you'll get the same outputs, but you don't want that in this project. Gobo's code will mix things up with some random numbers.

6 You need to add some more blocks to create Gobo's answer. Gobo will reply in one of two ways, numbered 1 and 2.

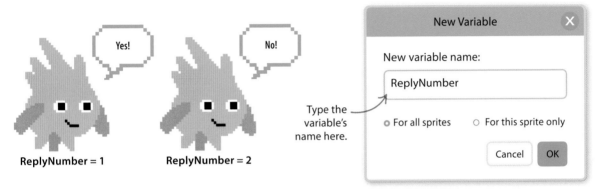

Yes!

No!

ReplyNumber = 1   **ReplyNumber = 2**

8 A small window will pop up. Type "ReplyNumber" into the box to name the new variable and click "OK".

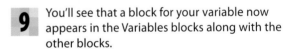

New Variable

New variable name:

ReplyNumber

Type the variable's name here.

○ For all sprites   ○ For this sprite only

Cancel   OK

7 The code will use a variable named "ReplyNumber" to store the number of the reply the program has chosen so it can show the correct message. To make a new variable, choose the orange Variables block at the bottom of the blocks palette, and click on the "Make a Variable" button.

Click here.

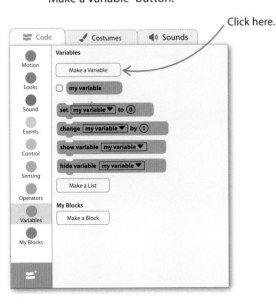

9 You'll see that a block for your variable now appears in the Variables blocks along with the other blocks.

If this check box is selected, the value of the variable is shown on the stage. Leave it checked for now.

This block is used to insert a value into the variable.

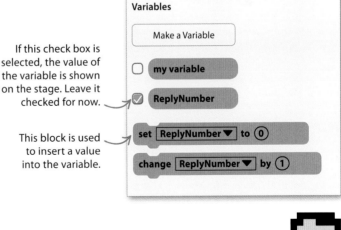

EXPERT TIPS

Random numbers

A random number is one that you can't predict before it appears. A die roll is a random number—any of the numbers from one to six could appear each time you roll the die. You don't know which number will come up until you roll. In Scratch, you can get a random number using the "pick random" block. Drag this block into the code area and experiment with it.

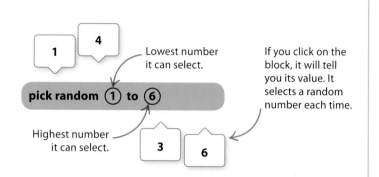

Lowest number it can select.

If you click on the block, it will tell you its value. It selects a random number each time.

pick random (1) to (6)

Highest number it can select.

10 The variable will hold the number of Gobo's reply, but the program needs a way to choose that number randomly. Add a "set my variable to" block to the bottom of Gobo's code. Open the block's drop-down menu and select "ReplyNumber". Then drag a green "pick random" block into it from the Operators section. Change the second number to 2. The green block picks randomly between 1 and 2, like flipping a coin.

set [ReplyNumber ▼] to ◯

pick random (1) to (2)

Change the second number to 2.

11 Next, create this block to add to the bottom of the code. It will make Gobo say "Yes!" if the value in the variable "ReplyNumber" is 1. The "say" block runs only if the value is one; otherwise, it is skipped.

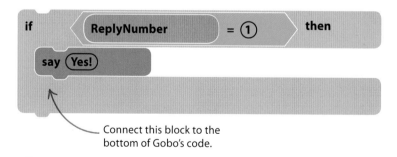

if   ReplyNumber = (1)   then

say (Yes!)

Connect this block to the bottom of Gobo's code.

12 Now run the project a few times. Around half of the time, Gobo will say "Yes!" The other times, it doesn't say anything. If you look at the top of the stage, you'll see the "ReplyNumber" variable says 1 when you get "Yes!" and 2 when you get no reply. Add this extra block to make Gobo say "No!" when the variable is 2.

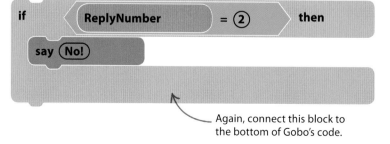

if   ReplyNumber = (2)   then

say (No!)

Again, connect this block to the bottom of Gobo's code.

13 The code should now look like this. Run the project a few times and make sure that Gobo gives random "yes" and "no" answers. If not, check all of the code carefully.

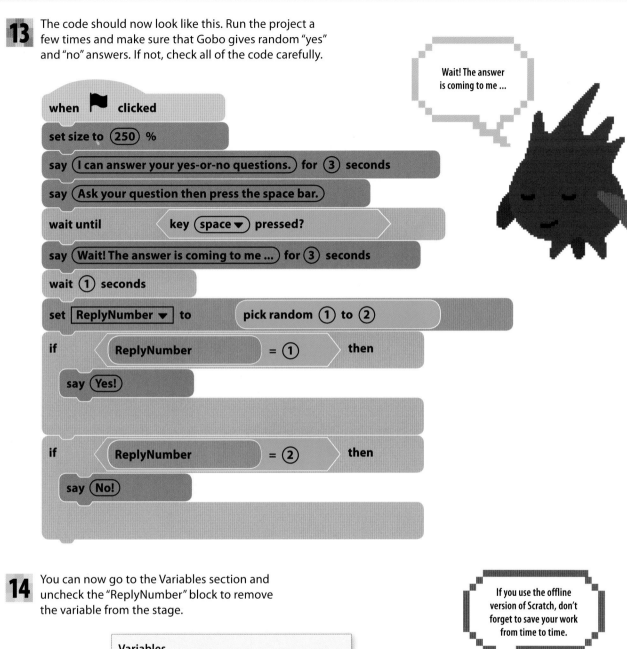

Wait! The answer is coming to me ...

14 You can now go to the Variables section and uncheck the "ReplyNumber" block to remove the variable from the stage.

If you use the offline version of Scratch, don't forget to save your work from time to time.

Uncheck the box.

Variables

Make a Variable

☐ **my variable**

☐ **ReplyNumber**

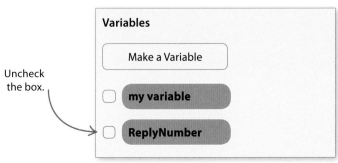

15 Now try using your project to answer some important questions to predict the future!

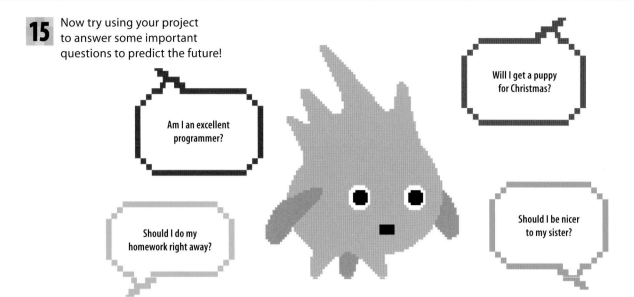

Will I get a puppy for Christmas?

Am I an excellent programmer?

Should I be nicer to my sister?

Should I do my homework right away?

More decisions

You've already seen how to use "if then" blocks containing questions to decide whether or not to run lines of code. In this project, you use green Operators blocks inside "if then" blocks to check the value of a variable. The pale blue question blocks have "yes" or "no" answers, but when you use the green blocks, you should ask if what they say is true or false.

There are three different green blocks you can use to compare numbers, each with a different job and symbol: = (equal to), > (greater than), and < (less than). Programmers call true-or-false decisions used inside "if then" blocks "Boolean conditions." They are named after the English mathematician George Boole (1815–1864).

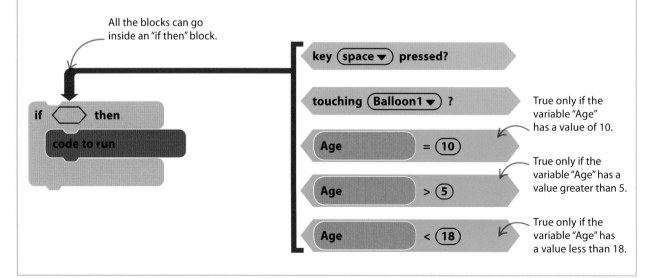

All the blocks can go inside an "if then" block.

if ⬡ then
   code to run

key (space ▼) pressed?

touching (Balloon1 ▼) ?

Age = 10
> True only if the variable "Age" has a value of 10.

Age > 5
> True only if the variable "Age" has a value greater than 5.

Age < 18
> True only if the variable "Age" has a value less than 18.

Hacks and tweaks

You can do much more with the random numbers than simply answering yes-or-no questions. Try exploring some of these possibilities.

▽ **Ask me another**

To make Gobo answer more questions after the first one, place the original code inside a "forever" loop, as shown here, with a few extra blocks to make Gobo prompt the user for a new question.

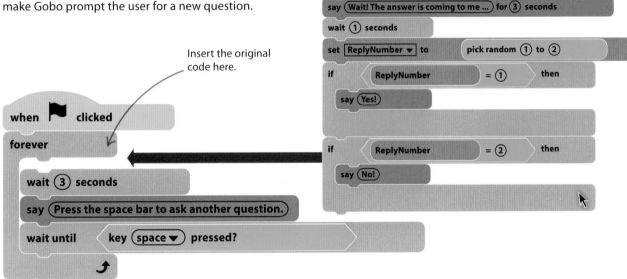

Insert the original code here.

```
set size to (250) %
say (I can answer your yes-or-no questions.) for (3) seconds
say (Ask your question then press the space bar.)
wait until          key (space ▼) pressed?
say (Wait! The answer is coming to me ...) for (3) seconds
wait (1) seconds
set  ReplyNumber ▼  to          pick random (1) to (2)
if          ReplyNumber          = (1)          then
    say (Yes!)

if          ReplyNumber          = (2)          then
    say (No!)
```

```
when ⚑ clicked
forever
    wait (3) seconds
    say (Press the space bar to ask another question.)
    wait until          key (space ▼) pressed?
```

▷ **Special effects**

You can alter Gobo's replies to be more fun. While you're at it, why not make Gobo change color or costume for each reply? You could also add sounds to its replies, some dance steps, or a spin.

How DARE you ask that!

```
if          ReplyNumber          = (2)          then
    say (How DARE you ask that!)
    switch costume to (gobo-c ▼)
    set  color ▼  effect to (50)
    start sound (Scream1 ▼)
```

▽ **More replies**

To add to the fun, you can extend the number of replies. You simply need to increase the top number in the "pick random" block to the new number of choices and then add extra "if then" blocks containing new "say" blocks. This example has six possible answers, but you can add as many as you like.

Change the 2 into a 6. This must match your number of replies or some responses will never appear.

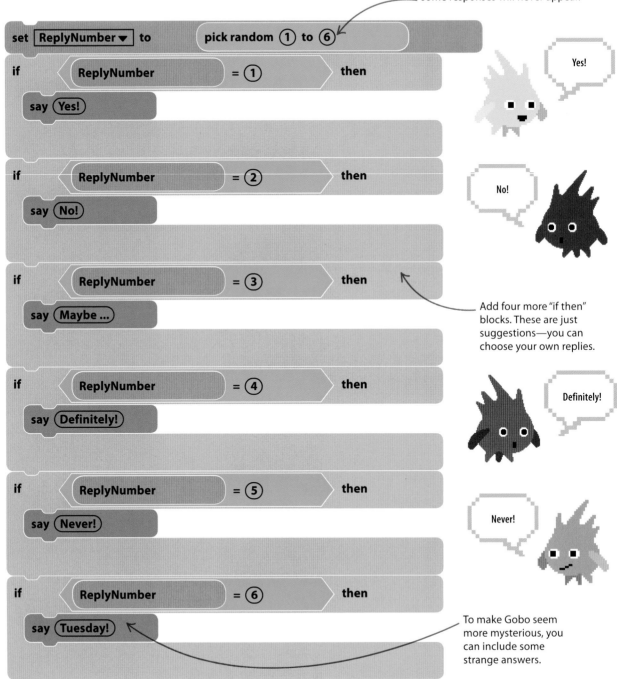

Add four more "if then" blocks. These are just suggestions—you can choose your own replies.

To make Gobo seem more mysterious, you can include some strange answers.

▽ Counting horse

You don't have to stick to yes-or-no answers—instead, you could answer questions like "How old am I?" or "What's my IQ?" with random numbers. Start a new project, load the Horse sprite, and add the code below to make it count out the answers by stomping up and down with its feet. You could also add some horse noises from the sound library.

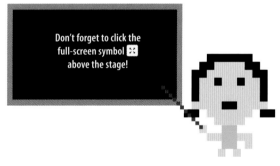

Don't forget to click the full-screen symbol ⬡ above the stage!

```
when 🏴 clicked
switch costume to (horse-a ▼)
say (I can answer your number questions.) for (3) seconds
say (Ask your question then press the space bar.)
wait until < key (space ▼) pressed >
say (Wait! The answer is coming to me ...) for (3) seconds
wait (1) seconds
set [ReplyNumber ▼] to (pick random (1) to (5))
repeat (ReplyNumber)
    switch costume to (horse-b ▼)
    wait (1) seconds
    switch costume to (horse-a ▼)
    wait (1) seconds
say (ReplyNumber)
```

Maximum number the horse can say.

This loop makes the horse count out the answer by lifting its feet.

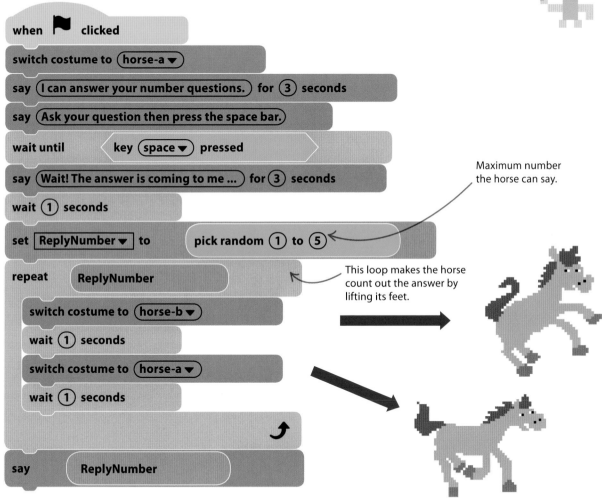

▷ Do as I say!

Instead of answering questions, Gobo could give random orders, such as "run up and down the stairs," "jump in the air twice," or "sing a famous song." Just change the text in the "say" blocks to Gobo's commands. You could also change Gobo's appearance to something grumpy to match the mood.

Take a hike!

Funny Faces

You can have lots of fun drawing your own sprites in Scratch—you don't have to stick to the ones in the sprites library. Creating your own sprites will give your projects a unique look. For this project, you can go wild making facial features and accessories to invent a wacky face.

How it works

This project starts with a blank face surrounded by a collection of eyes, noses, and other items that you can drag into the middle to create crazy expressions. Press the green flag to reset the face and start again.

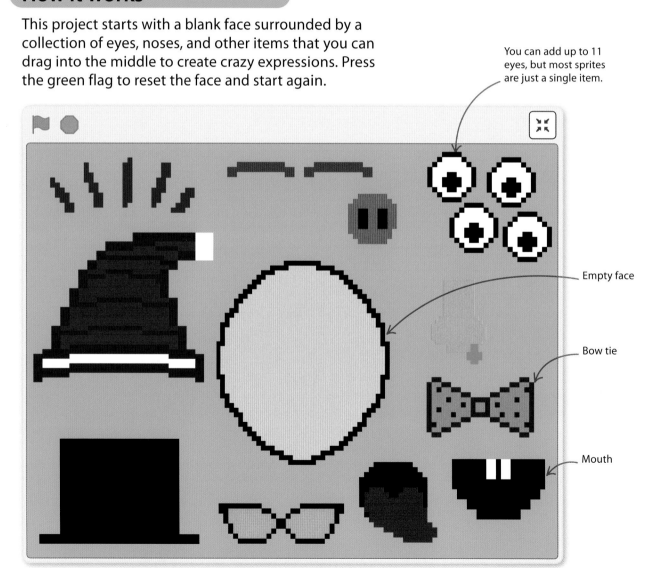

You can add up to 11 eyes, but most sprites are just a single item.

Empty face

Bow tie

Mouth

▷ **Funny, funnier, funniest!**
This project lets you use your creativity and
imagination to the fullest. You don't have
to make human faces. You can make aliens,
monsters, or anything!

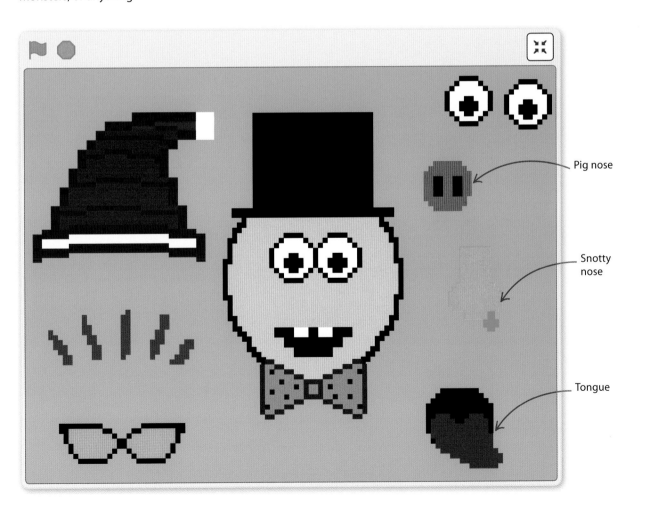

Pig nose

Snotty nose

Tongue

Get painting

Dust off your digital overalls because it's time for some painting. Scratch has a great paint editor built in, so you have all the tools you need to create a mini-masterpiece for each body part and item of clothing.

1 Start a new project and remove the cat sprite by right-clicking on it in the sprites list and selecting "delete". You're going to make your own sprites, so click on the paint symbol ✔ in the sprites menu to create the first one.

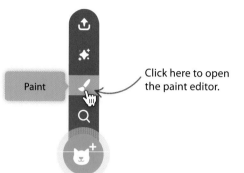

Paint

Click here to open the paint editor.

2 Scratch's paint editor will now open. You can use the paint editor to draw your own sprites. Make sure "Convert to Bitmap" is selected in the bottom left.

Undo

Redo

Costume   costume1

Selected color

Fill   10

Brush tool   Line tool

Circle tool   Rectangle tool

Text tool   Use this tool to fill a shape with color.

Eraser   Use this tool to select part of a drawing.

Convert to Vector

3 Click on the brush tool in the upper-left corner of the paint editor. Then click and draw an oval shape to form the head for your funny face. The middle should be near the small cross in the center of the painting area.

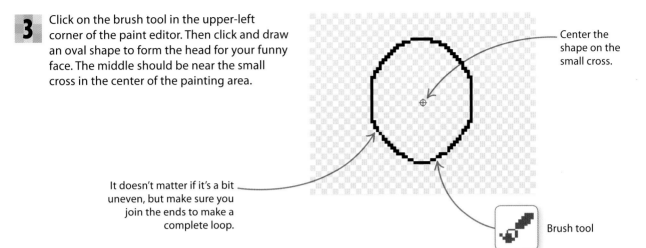

Center the shape on the small cross.

It doesn't matter if it's a bit uneven, but make sure you join the ends to make a complete loop.

Brush tool

4 Now choose the fill tool, which looks like a bucket of paint being tipped over. Click on the "Fill" tab at the top left to choose a color for the face. Then click inside the head to fill it with your chosen color.

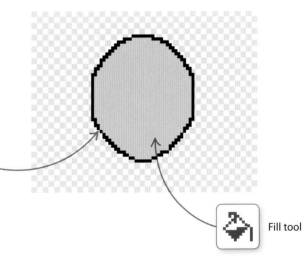

If the color accidentally fills the checked background area, click the undo button and check the outline of the face for gaps.

Fill tool

Change name here.

5 Well done—you've created a head! As a finishing touch, change the name of this sprite from "Sprite1" to "Head" in the information panel above the sprites list.

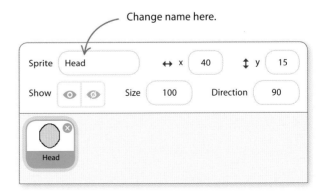

| Sprite | Head | | ↔ x | 40 | ↕ y | 15 |
| Show | 👁 🚫 | Size | 100 | Direction | 90 |

Head

6 The head needs to be in the center of the stage when the Funny Face project runs. The project will position every sprite on the screen at the start to keep things tidy. To do this for the head, click on the Code tab and drag these blocks to the code area.

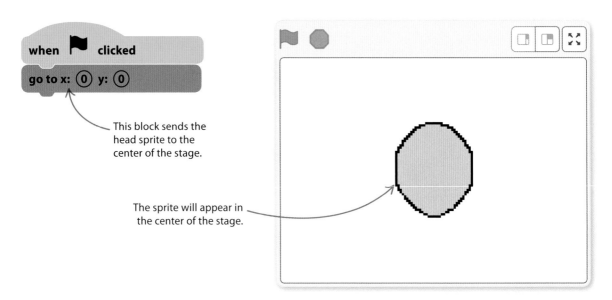

when 🏳 clicked

go to x: ⓪ y: ⓪

This block sends the head sprite to the center of the stage.

The sprite will appear in the center of the stage.

Coordinates

To pinpoint any spot on the stage, you can use two numbers called coordinates. The x coordinate, written first, tells you how far the point is across the stage horizontally. The y coordinate, written second, tells you how far the point is up or down the stage vertically. The x coordinates go from –240 to 240. The y coordinates go from –180 to 180. The coordinates of a point are written as (x, y). The center of the bow tie on the right, for instance, has the coordinates (215, 90).

Every spot on the stage has a unique pair of coordinates that can be used to position a sprite exactly.

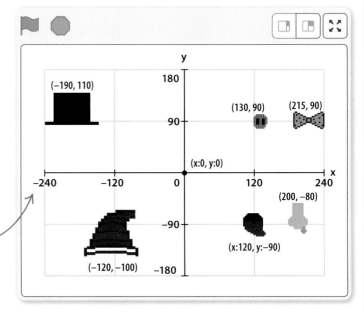

Time to make lots of sprites

The more different eyes, noses, mouths, ears, hats, and accessories your Funny Face project has, the more silly faces you can make, so spend some time making as many as you can. It's great fun. You can also find useful items in Scratch's costumes library, such as hats and sunglasses. You can skip the drawing stages for those.

7 Follow steps 7–11 to create your own items. Click on the paint symbol ✔ in the sprites menu to create the new sprite. Use the paint editor tools to draw it, following the tips shown on this page.

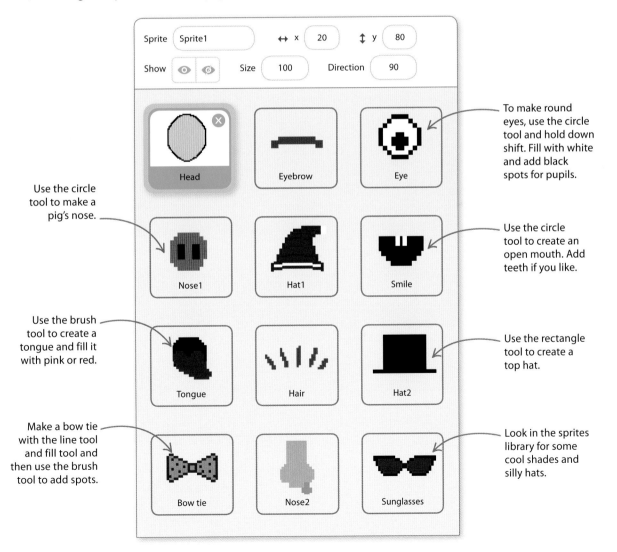

| Sprite | Sprite1 | ↔ x | 20 | ↕ y | 80 |

Show 👁 ⬷ Size 100 Direction 90

To make round eyes, use the circle tool and hold down shift. Fill with white and add black spots for pupils.

Use the circle tool to make a pig's nose.

Use the circle tool to create an open mouth. Add teeth if you like.

Use the brush tool to create a tongue and fill it with pink or red.

Use the rectangle tool to create a top hat.

Make a bow tie with the line tool and fill tool and then use the brush tool to add spots.

Look in the sprites library for some cool shades and silly hats.

Head Eyebrow Eye
Nose1 Hat1 Smile
Tongue Hair Hat2
Bow tie Nose2 Sunglasses

8 Click on each sprite in the sprites list and give your creation a meaningful name.

Type a name for the sprite here.

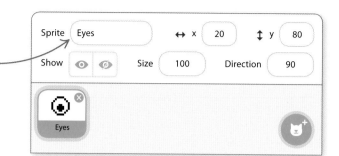

9 When you've finished drawing a sprite, drag it across the stage to its starting position outside the face. Don't worry if the sprites overlap a bit.

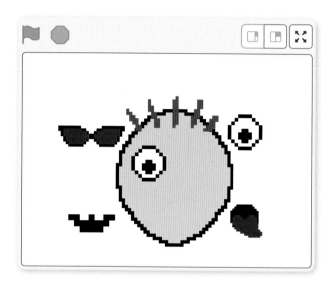

10 To make the new sprite appear in the right place when you run the project, use the mouse to drag it to its start position and then give it some code like this. The "go to" block in the blocks palette will automatically show the sprite's current coordinates.

```
when 🏴 clicked
go to x: 150 y: 100
```

Drag this block in from the Motion blocks, and it will already contain the correct coordinates.

11 Go back to step 7 and repeat the process until you have all the sprites you want.

Hey, this is a loop!

12 Now add a plain backdrop. Look in the stage info area to the right of the sprites list and click on "Choose a Backdrop". Select the paint symbol ✏ to paint a new backdrop. Then choose a color from the palette, and use the fill tool to fill the entire white area.

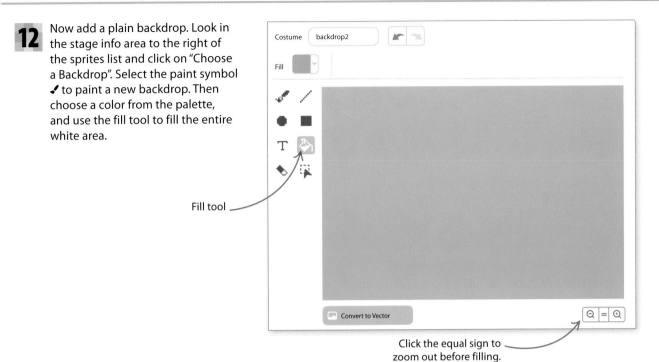

Fill tool

Click the equal sign to zoom out before filling.

Clones

You might want to use some sprites lots of times—perhaps your face will be funnier with 10 eyes instead of two. Scratch allows you to "clone" a sprite to make fully working copies.

13 Make 10 clones of the eye sprite by adding this loop to its code. Now when you run the project, you can place all 11 eyes!

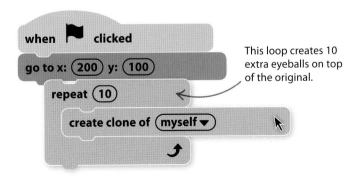

This loop creates 10 extra eyeballs on top of the original.

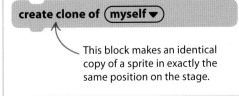

Hacks and tweaks

Funny Faces is lots of fun to extend. Create more silly sprites and think about how to make them move. As a finishing touch, you can frame your creation!

▽ **Special effects**

Can't see the eyes through the glasses? No problem—make the sunglasses transparent with Scratch's ghost effect. You'll find the block in the Looks section, where it's called "set color effect to". Change "color" to "ghost" in its menu.

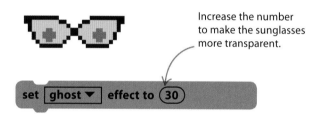

Increase the number to make the sunglasses more transparent.

`set ghost ▼ effect to (30)`

▽ **Spinning tie**

Bring your sprites to life by making them move. To make the bow tie spin around, add a "forever" loop containing a "turn" block.

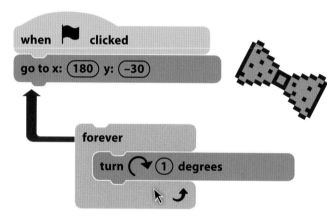

```
when ⚑ clicked
go to x: (180) y: (-30)

forever
    turn ↻ (1) degrees
```

▽ **Snotty nose**

To make disgusting green snot drip out of the nose, create two new costumes for the nose with spots of green color. Then add these new blocks to make the snot drip.

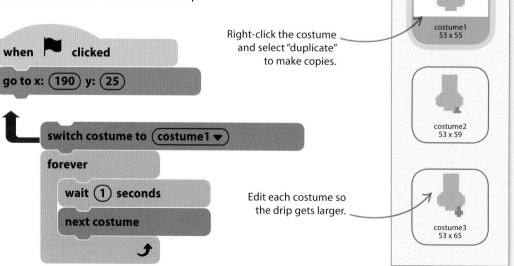

```
when ⚑ clicked
go to x: (190) y: (25)

switch costume to (costume1 ▼)
forever
    wait (1) seconds
    next costume
```

Right-click the costume and select "duplicate" to make copies.

costume1
53 x 55

costume2
53 x 59

Edit each costume so the drip gets larger.

costume3
53 x 65

In the frame

To create a neat frame around your funny face, follow these steps.

1 Click the paint symbol ✔ in the sprites menu to create a new sprite in the paint editor. Before you start painting, open the Code tab and give the sprite these code blocks. They hide the frame at the start and make it appear when you press the space bar and disappear when you press the "c" key.

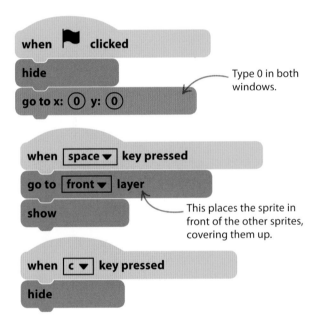

Type 0 in both windows.

This places the sprite in front of the other sprites, covering them up.

2 Run the project to center the sprite. Next, click the Costumes tab to return to the paint editor. Choose black in the color panel, and use the fill tool to fill the white area with black. Then use the select tool to draw a rectangle in the middle, and press "delete" on your keyboard to make a hole. Check the stage to see whether the frame is the right shape, and adjust as needed.

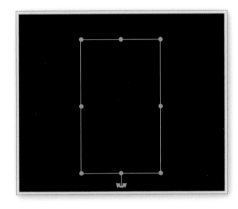

Select tool — Fill tool

3 Now run the project. Make a silly face and then see whether you can make the frame appear and disappear with the space bar and "c" key.

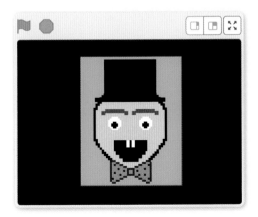

TRY THIS

Try something different

You can use this project to create anything from snowmen and Christmas trees to monsters and aliens!

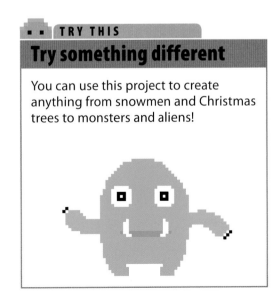

Art

Birthday Card

Who wants an ordinary birthday card when you can have an animated feast for the eyes and ears? Scratch is the perfect tool for making a birthday card. This card has singing sharks, but you can adapt the project to make someone a unique card.

A balloon-filled backdrop sets the scene.

How it works

When you run this project, a mysterious flashing green button appears. Press the button, and an animated birthday card fills the screen, complete with singing sharks. The sharks take turns singing the lines of the "Happy Birthday" song.

HAPPY

Happy birthday to you!

PRESS ONLY ON YOUR BIRTHDAY!

Click the button to open the birthday card.

The sharks drop in from the top and then sing "Happy Birthday."

The animated sign at the top rocks from side to side.

Be sure to run this project in full-screen mode.

△ **Gliding around**
This project uses the "glide" block, which makes sprites move smoothly around the stage. You need to use Scratch's coordinates system to set the exact start and finish point of each glide. If you can't remember how coordinates work, see the Funny Faces project.

△ **Keeping time**
Like Animal Race, this project uses messages sent from one sprite to another to control the timing of code blocks. The singing sharks send messages back and forth to time their lines of "Happy Birthday."

The cake slides into view from the edge of the stage.

Birthday button

To avoid spoiling the surprise of the card, all that appears when the project is run is a message and a button for the birthday person to press.

1 Start a new project. Remove the cat sprite by right-clicking on it in the sprites list and selecting "delete". Load the Button1 sprite from the sprites library.

Button1

3 To add the sign saying PRESS ONLY ON YOUR BIRTHDAY!, you need to edit the backdrop. First select the stage by clicking the small white rectangle to the right of the sprites list. Then click the Backdrops tab above the blocks palette.

2 Add these two code blocks to Button1. The first one makes the button appear in the center of the stage and flash invitingly when the project starts. The second one runs after the button is clicked, making the button disappear and sending a message to launch the rest of the card. After adding the "broadcast" block, open its drop-down menu, choose "New message", and call the message "Go!"

This block positions the button in the center of the stage.

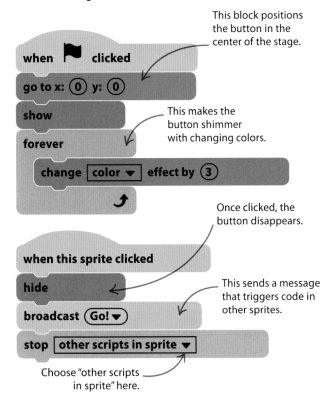

```
when [flag] clicked
go to x: (0) y: (0)
show
forever
    change [color ▼] effect by (3)
```

This makes the button shimmer with changing colors.

Once clicked, the button disappears.

```
when this sprite clicked
hide
broadcast (Go! ▼)
stop [other scripts in sprite ▼]
```

This sends a message that triggers code in other sprites.

Choose "other scripts in sprite" here.

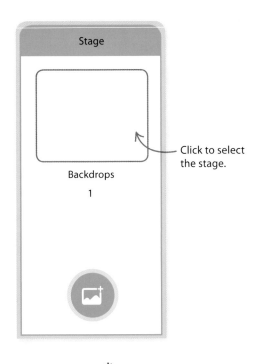

Stage

Backdrops
1

Click to select the stage.

Surprise!

4 Scratch's paint editor will now open. Choose the text tool T and click in the large white area, about a third of the way down. Type the words PRESS ONLY ON YOUR BIRTHDAY! If you want to retype the message for any reason, use the select tool to draw a box around the text, and press delete on your keyboard before starting again.

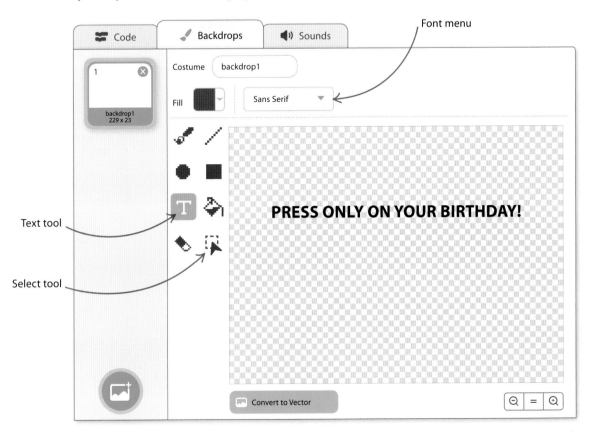

Font menu

Text tool

Select tool

5 You can choose a font using the font menu at the top of the paint editor. "Sans Serif" works well for a birthday card.

You can choose any font you like.

6 Use the select tool to resize or move the text until you're happy with it.

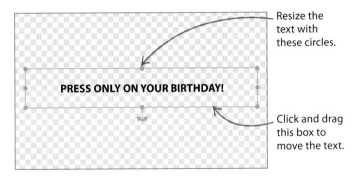

Resize the text with these circles.

Click and drag this box to move the text.

7 For the card itself, you need a different backdrop. Click the backdrop symbol ⬚ in the lower right of the Scratch window to choose a new backdrop from the library. Then select the "party" backdrop.

Click here to open the backdrops library.

Choose a Backdrop

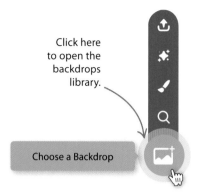

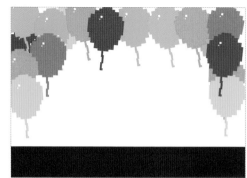

8 Make sure you still have the stage selected in the lower right of the Scratch window and not one of the sprites. Click on the Code tab above the blocks palette, and add these code blocks for the stage. Now try running the project and see what happens when you click the button.

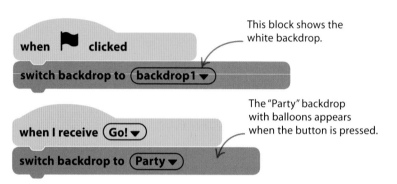

This block shows the white backdrop.

The "Party" backdrop with balloons appears when the button is pressed.

when 🏴 clicked
switch backdrop to (backdrop1 ▼)

when I receive (Go! ▼)
switch backdrop to (Party ▼)

Enter the cake

Once the button is pressed, the card opens. The button's code broadcasts the "Go!" message to all the sprites to trigger the animations and music.

9 What else does a birthday need besides a card? A cake! Click on the sprite symbol 🐱 in the sprites list, and add the Cake sprite to the project.

Cake

10 If you look in the Sounds tab at the top of the Scratch window, you'll see that the "Birthday" sound has already been loaded.

≋ Code   ✏ Costumes   ◀)) Sounds

1 ◀))
Birthday
7.32

Sound   Birthday

11 We want the cake to slide in from the left, starting from a position offstage. If we send the cake to the edge of the stage (–240, –100), half of it will show because that's the position of the cake's center. You can't send a sprite completely off the screen, so we'll send it to (–300, –100) so that only a tiny bit shows.

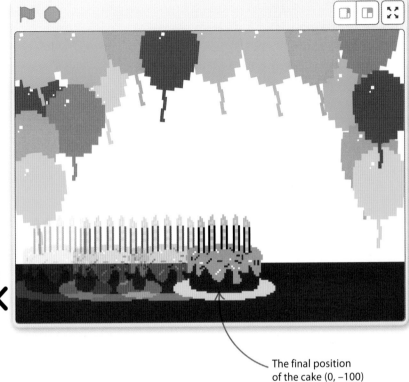

The starting position of the cake (–300, –100)

The final position of the cake (0, –100)

12 Add these code blocks to the cake to hide it when the project runs, and then make it glide in from the left when the green button is pressed. Note that the cake broadcasts a new message, called "Line1". Later, you'll use this to make one of the sharks sing the first line of "Happy Birthday."

This is the cake's starting position off the left of the stage.

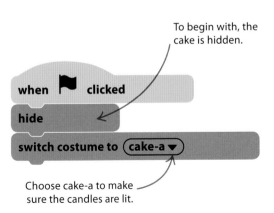

To begin with, the cake is hidden.

when 🏳 clicked
hide
switch costume to (cake-a ▼)

Choose cake-a to make sure the candles are lit.

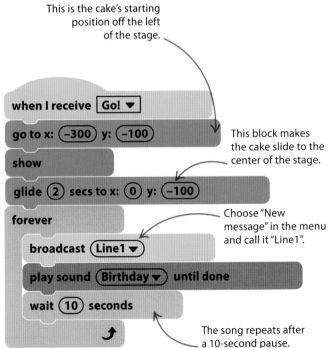

when I receive (Go! ▼)
go to x: (–300) y: (–100)
show
glide (2) secs to x: (0) y: (–100)
forever
  broadcast (Line1 ▼)
  play sound (Birthday ▼) until done
  wait (10) seconds

This block makes the cake slide to the center of the stage.

Choose "New message" in the menu and call it "Line1".

The song repeats after a 10-second pause.

Birthday banner

The next thing needed for a party atmosphere is an animated birthday banner that rocks back and forth.

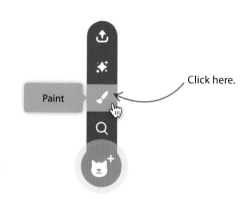

Click here.

Paint

13 The banner will be a sprite, but this time you'll create a new sprite by painting it instead of loading it from the library. Click the paint symbol ✎ in the sprites menu, and the paint editor will open. A new sprite will appear in the sprites list. Rename the sprite "Banner".

14 Draw your birthday banner in the paint editor. Make sure you select "Convert to Bitmap". Use the rectangle tool to create the banner, either as a solid color or just an outline. Then use the text tool to add the words HAPPY BIRTHDAY! Try whichever font and colors you like. Use the select tool to position the text or trim the banner to fit.

HAPPY BIRTHDAY

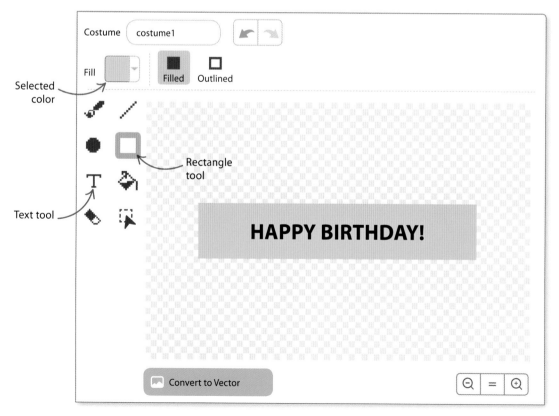

Costume | costume1

Fill | Filled | Outlined

Selected color

Rectangle tool

Text tool

HAPPY BIRTHDAY!

Convert to Vector

15 Now select the Code tab and add the banner's two code blocks. These keep it hidden until the button is pressed and then jiggle the banner around. Run the project to make sure it works.

The banner starts off tipped a little counterclockwise.

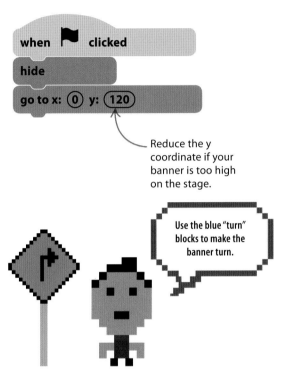

```
when 🏳 clicked
hide
go to x: 0 y: 120
```

Reduce the y coordinate if your banner is too high on the stage.

Use the blue "turn" blocks to make the banner turn.

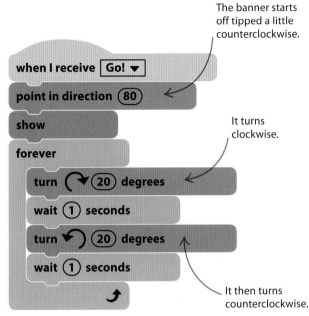

```
when I receive Go! ▼
point in direction 80
show
forever
    turn ↻ 20 degrees
    wait 1 seconds
    turn ↺ 20 degrees
    wait 1 seconds
```

It turns clockwise.

It then turns counterclockwise.

EXPERT TIPS

Directions

Scratch uses degrees to set the direction of sprites. You can choose any number from −179° to 180°. Remember, negative numbers point sprites left, and positive numbers point them right. Use 0° to go straight up and 180° to go straight down.

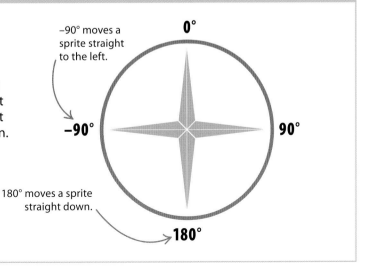

−90° moves a sprite straight to the left.

0°

−90°

90°

180° moves a sprite straight down.

180°

Singing sharks

What's the perfect finishing touch to a birthday surprise?
Yes, of course—singing sharks! The two sharks will take
turns singing by sending messages to each other after
each line of the song.

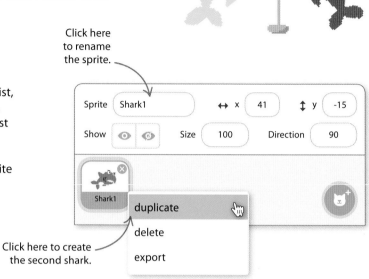

Click here
to rename
the sprite.

16 Click the sprite symbol 🐱 in the sprites list,
and add the Shark2 sprite to the project.
You'll need two sharks, so rename the first
one Shark1. To create the second shark,
right-click (or control-click) on the first
shark and select "duplicate". The new sprite
will be named Shark2 automatically.

| Sprite | Shark1 | ↔ x | 41 | ↕ y | -15 |

| Show | 👁 ◎ | Size | 100 | Direction | 90 |

Shark1

duplicate

delete

export

Click here to create
the second shark.

17 Now give Shark1 this code. When the project
runs, Shark1 is hidden but takes its position in
the top left of the stage. When it receives the
"Go!" message, it reveals itself and glides down
to the bottom of the stage.

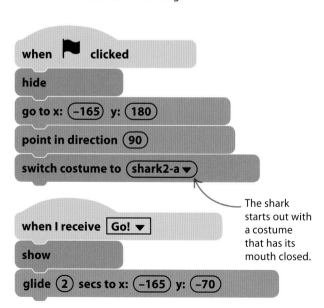

when 🚩 clicked

hide

go to x: (-165) y: (180)

point in direction (90)

switch costume to (shark2-a ▼)

when I receive (Go! ▼)

show

glide (2) secs to x: (-165) y: (-70)

The shark
starts out with
a costume
that has its
mouth closed.

18 Add this code to Shark2. Run
the project to test the sharks.

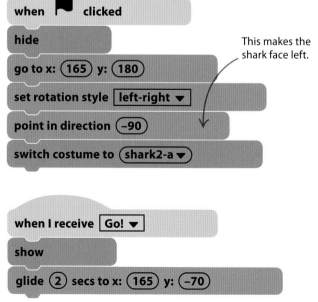

when 🚩 clicked

hide

go to x: (165) y: (180)

set rotation style [left-right ▼]

point in direction (-90)

switch costume to (shark2-a ▼)

This makes the
shark face left.

when I receive (Go! ▼)

show

glide (2) secs to x: (165) y: (-70)

19 Time to get the sharks singing. Remember the loop belonging to the cake sprite that plays "Happy Birthday"? It sends the message "Line1" every time the song starts. Add the code shown on the left to Shark1 and the code on the right to Shark2 to make them react to the message. More messages make them take turns to sing each line. You'll need to create new messages for each line of the song. Name them by using the drop-down menu in the "broadcast" blocks.

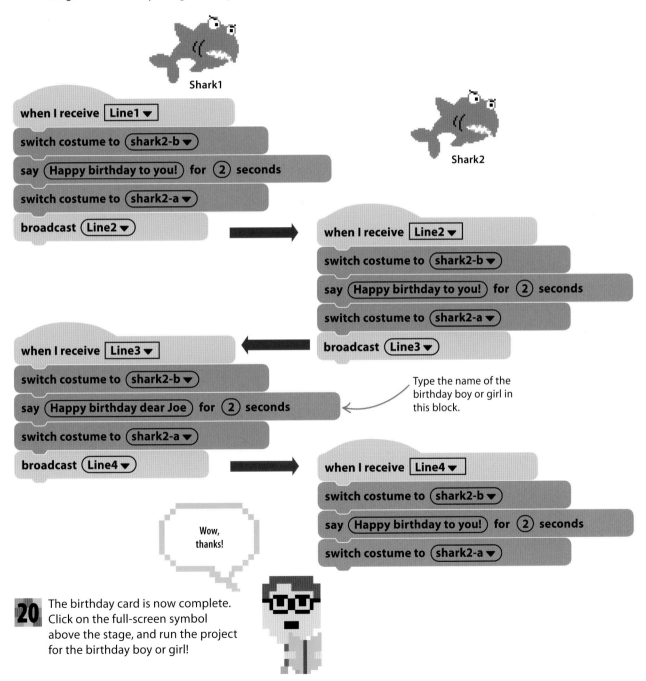

Type the name of the birthday boy or girl in this block.

Wow, thanks!

20 The birthday card is now complete. Click on the full-screen symbol above the stage, and run the project for the birthday boy or girl!

Hacks and tweaks

You can customize your card for different people and occasions. Instead of using singing sharks, you could try singing lions, penguins, elephants, or ghosts. Change the song to "Merry Christmas" or "Jingle Bells," and replace the balloons with snowy Christmas trees if you like. Feel free to experiment.

▽ **Fading in**

The sharks drop from the top when they appear, but you can use Scratch's special effects to create a more dramatic entrance. To make an invisible sprite fade in slowly, for instance, use the "set ghost effect" block in the code shown here.

▽ **Supersize your sprite**

Another way to make a dramatic entrance is to start tiny and grow into a giant. Put a "change size by" block in a "repeat" loop to create this effect. You could also try making your sprite spin as it grows, or add a "change whirl effect" block to turn it into a crazy whirlpool.

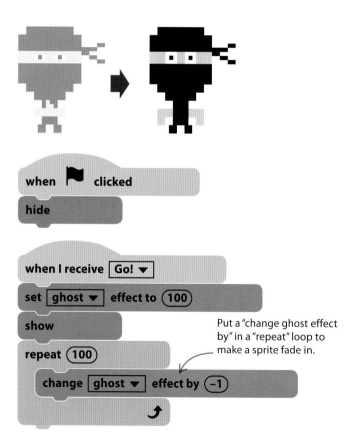

Put a "change ghost effect by" in a "repeat" loop to make a sprite fade in.

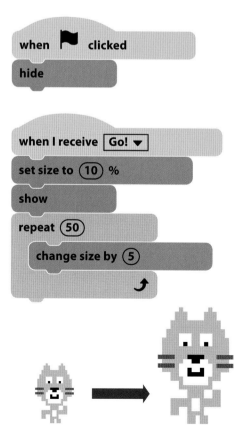

△ Adding photos

Why not try importing a photo of the birthday boy or girl into the project? You can upload any picture you like to make a new sprite by clicking the upload symbol ⬆ in the sprites menu. But don't share projects containing people's photos without their permission.

Happy birthday to you ...

●● TRY THIS

Sharks on elastic!

See if you can figure out how to make the sharks move up at the end of the "Happy Birthday" song and then come back down when it's time to sing again. Don't forget to work on a separate copy of your project so you won't lose the original if things go wrong.

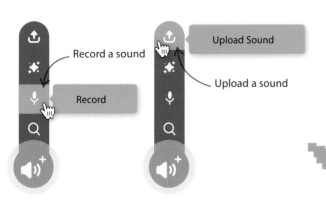

Record a sound

Record

Upload Sound

Upload a sound

△ Adding sound

You don't have to use Scratch's built-in sounds and songs—you can add your own music or record your very own version of "Happy Birthday" if you want. Click the upload symbol ⬆ in the sounds menu to add a sound file from your computer. Click the microphone symbol 🎤 to record your own sounds.

△ Birthday dancers

Why not reuse some of your dancers from the Dino Dance Party in your birthday card? If you do, adjust the timing of the costume change so they dance in time to the music.

Spiralizer

Try out this spinning spiral project. Change the patterns using special sliders to alter the values of variables in the code. You control the art—the possibilities are endless!

How it works

This simple project has only one sprite: a colored ball, which stays in the middle. Scratch's clone blocks make copies of the ball that move outward in straight lines. A spiral pattern forms because each clone moves in a slightly different direction, like water from a garden sprinkler. The Scratch pen draws a trail behind each clone, making colorful background patterns.

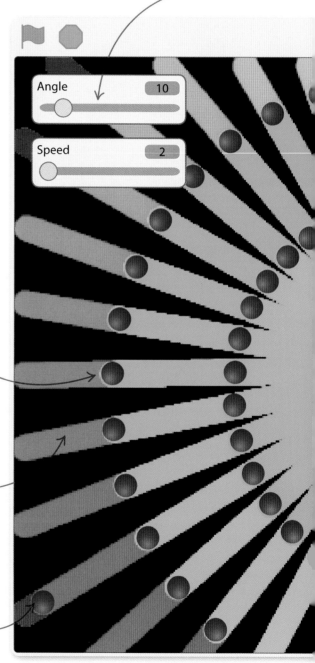

Adjust the sliders to change the look of the spiral.

Angle 10

Speed 2

The clones' different directions make them form a spiral.

Each line is drawn using Scratch's Pen extension, which lets any sprite draw.

Each cloned ball flies in a straight line from the center to the edge.

Wow! This project has got me in a spin.

The ball in the center is the original sprite; all the others are clones.

Click this icon to switch from full-screen mode to editor mode.

△ **Clones**
Clones are working copies of sprites. When a clone is created, it appears on top of the existing sprite and has the same properties, such as direction and size.

△ **Scratch pen**
Every sprite can draw a trail behind it wherever it goes—just add the dark green "pen down" block to its code. By adding the Pen extension, you get extra blocks added to the blocks palette to change the pen's color, shade, and thickness.

Ball clones

Scratch allows you to create hundreds of clones from a single sprite, filling the stage with action. Each clone is a fully working copy of the original sprite but also runs some special code that affects only clones.

1 Start a new project. Remove the cat sprite by right-clicking on it and selecting "delete". Load the ball sprite from the sprites library. The ball has several different colored costumes. Click the Costumes tab, and choose the color you like best.

Ball

2 Add this loop to make clones of the ball. When you run this code, nothing much will appear to happen. Actually, it's making lots of clones of the ball sprite, but they're all on top of each other. You can drag them apart with the mouse (but only in editor mode, not full-screen mode).

3 To make the clones move, add this code to the ball sprite. Every new clone will now run its own copy of this code when it appears. The code makes the clone move away from the center in the direction the parent sprite was pointing when it was cloned. Run the project.

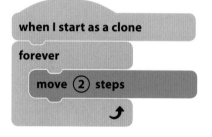

```
when I start as a clone
forever
    move 2 steps
```

▷ **What's going on?**
The parent sprite changes its direction a little before each clone is created. As a result, the clones move off in slightly different directions, one after another. Each clone travels in a straight line to the edge of the stage, making the clones form an ever-expanding spiral pattern.

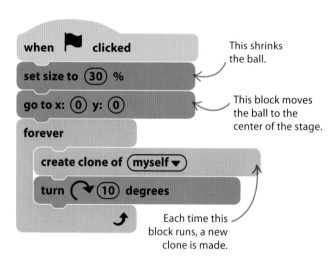

```
when [flag] clicked
set size to 30 %
go to x: 0 y: 0
forever
    create clone of myself
    turn ↻ 10 degrees
```

This shrinks the ball.

This block moves the ball to the center of the stage.

Each time this block runs, a new clone is made.

4 The clones stop appearing after a while because Scratch won't allow more than 300 clones on the stage at once. Any instructions to make new clones after this are ignored. The clones stop forming at the center, and all the existing clones collect around the edge of the stage.

The clones collect at the edge because the "move" block can't take a sprite completely off the stage.

Once there are 300 clones on the stage, no more clones are created.

5 To fix this problem, add an "if then" block inside the clone's "move" loop to delete the clone when it gets to the edge. Run this version. Now the balls should disappear at the edge as fast as they are made, and the spiral should continue for as long as you want—Scratch will never reach its clone limit.

6 To make the spiral show up better, add a black background. Click the paint symbol ✏ in the backdrops menu to the right of the sprites list to create a new backdrop. Use the fill tool to paint the backdrop solid black.

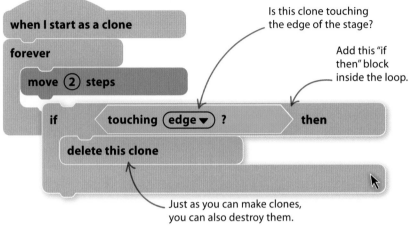

Is this clone touching the edge of the stage?

Add this "if then" block inside the loop.

Just as you can make clones, you can also destroy them.

Taking control

There are two numbers in the ball's code that you can change to alter the spiral's appearance. One is the change in the angle before each new clone appears. The other is the number of steps in the "move" block, which determines the clones' speed. If you create variables for these numbers, Scratch lets you add a slider control to the stage so you can change them while the project is running. This makes experimenting easy.

Click here to open the "New Variable" window.

Type the variable's name here.

7 Select the ball sprite in the sprites list. Choose Variables in the blocks palette, and then use the "Make a Variable" button to create two variables: "Angle" and "Speed".

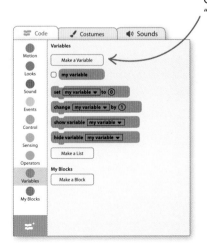

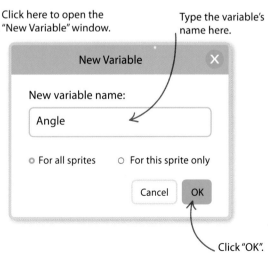

New variable name:

Angle

○ For all sprites   ○ For this sprite only

Cancel   OK

Click "OK".

8 Keep the variables checked in the blocks palette so that they appear on the stage.

The variables are shown on the stage like this.

Variables

Make a Variable

☑ **Angle**

☐ **my variable**

☑ **Speed**

Leave the checks in these boxes.

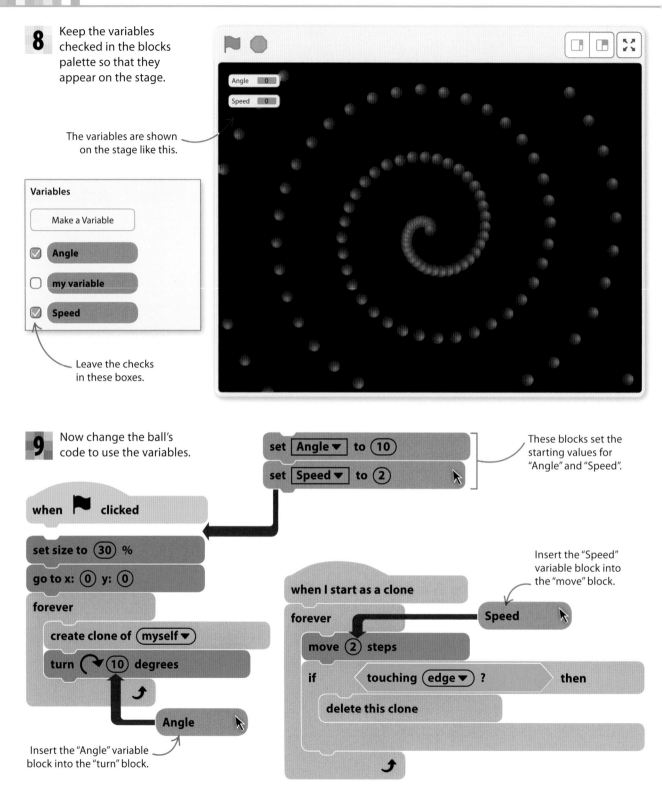

9 Now change the ball's code to use the variables.

set Angle ▼ to (10)

set Speed ▼ to (2)

These blocks set the starting values for "Angle" and "Speed".

when ⚑ clicked

set size to (30) %

go to x: (0) y: (0)

forever

   create clone of (myself ▼)

   turn ↻ (10) degrees

Angle

Insert the "Angle" variable block into the "turn" block.

Insert the "Speed" variable block into the "move" block.

when I start as a clone

forever

   move (2) steps

   if ⟨ touching (edge ▼) ? ⟩ then

      delete this clone

Speed

10 Run the project, and everything should work just as before. Right-click on the "Angle" variable on the stage and select "slider". Do the same for "Speed".

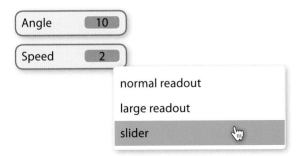

11 Both variables will now have a slider control. The sliders let you instantly change the values stored in the variables. Run the project and try moving the sliders. The patterns of the ball clones will change instantly.

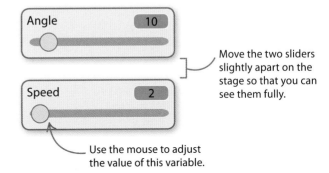

Move the two sliders slightly apart on the stage so that you can see them fully.

Use the mouse to adjust the value of this variable.

12 Now try experimenting with different values.

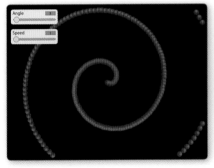

Angle 3, Speed 1

Angle 3, Speed 30

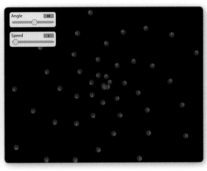

Angle 49, Speed 5

When the space bar is pressed, every clone runs this code and deletes itself.

13 You might find it handy to clear the stage of clones from time to time, so add this code to turn the space bar into a clone destroyer. Each clone runs all the ball sprite's code except the one headed by a green flag, so this code will affect every clone. Run the project, and tap the space bar to try it out.

```
when space ▼ key pressed
delete this clone
```

The mighty pen

Scratch has extensions—extra blocks of code that can be added to projects. One of these extensions is a magic pen. If you switch the pen on, it will draw a line wherever the sprite goes. Every clone has a pen, too, so by turning them on you can create some amazing art.

14 To add the extra Pen blocks, click "Add Extension" at the bottom left of the screen and choose "Pen". Add these green blocks to activate the pen for every clone.

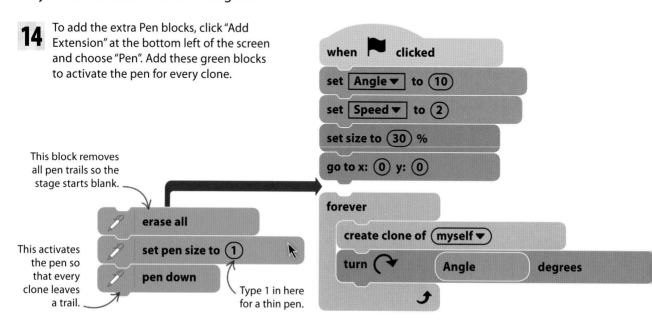

This block removes all pen trails so the stage starts blank.

This activates the pen so that every clone leaves a trail.

Type 1 in here for a thin pen.

15 Run the project to see a beautiful display. You can use the sliders to try different numbers. Odd numbers work well for "Angle"—try 7 or 11—because the whole pattern moves around a little each time, filling the space and creating interesting effects.

When many lines are drawn close to each other, imperfections line up and make strange swirls called "Moiré patterns."

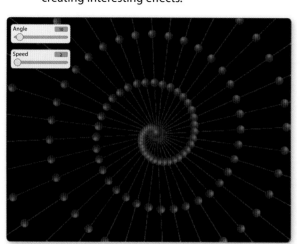

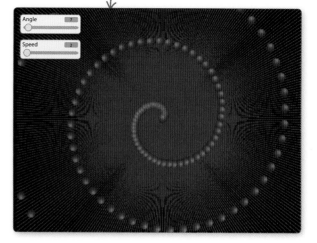

16 Add an "erase all" block to your clone-destroyer code. This makes the space bar wipe the stage clear of everything, creating a blank canvas for your art.

when [space ▼] key pressed

delete this clone

✏ erase all

Insert an "erase all" block here to remove all pen traces from the stage.

17 As a final experiment, change the pen color for each clone so that each one draws in a new color.

when ⚑ clicked

set [Angle ▼] to (10)

set [Speed ▼] to (2)

set size to (30) %

go to x: (0) y: (0)

✏ erase all

✏ set pen size to (1)

✏ pen down

forever

   create clone of (myself ▼)

   turn ↻ (Angle) degrees

✏ change pen (color ▼) by (1)

Insert this block to change the pen color for each clone.

Angle | 10
Speed | 2

I can spin a rainbow!

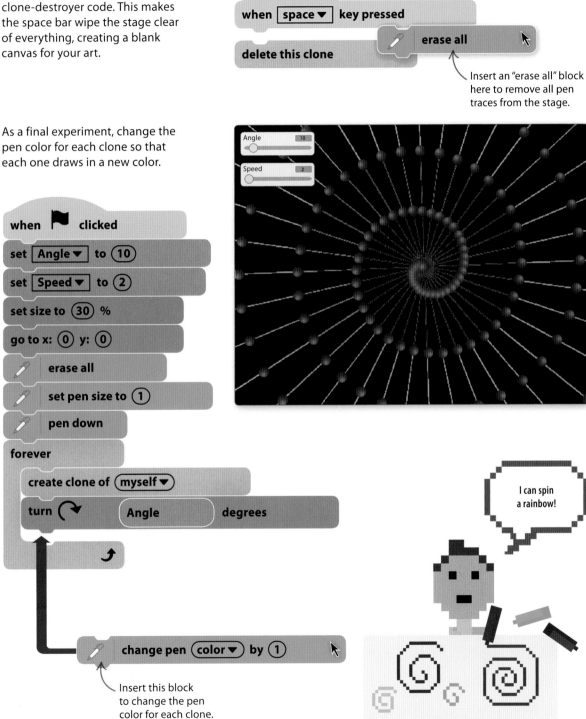

18 Run the project and explore the range of effects you can create by changing the sliders, the pen size, and the pen's color. Try thicker pen sizes and see what happens. Don't forget you can clear up by pressing the space bar.

Play with the sliders to see what stunning visual effects you can make.

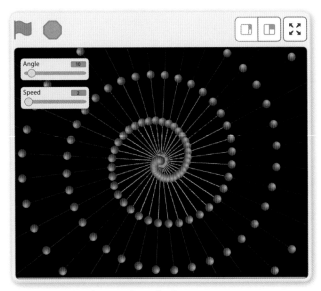

Pen size = 1, Angle = 10, Speed = 2

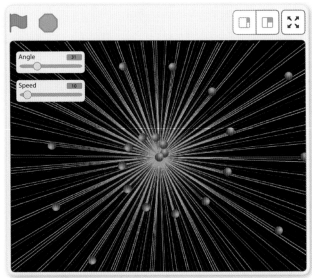

Pen size = 1, Angle = 31, Speed = 10

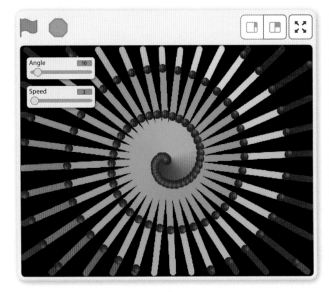

Pen size = 10, Angle = 10, Speed = 2

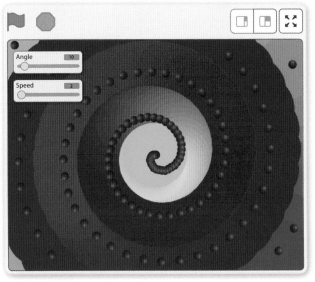

Pen size = 100, Angle = 10, Speed = 2

Hacks and tweaks

The spiral generator is perfect for customizing. Here are some more suggestions for changes, but don't be afraid to experiment with the code and try your own ideas. You could even adapt the project to make a game in which the player's sprite has to dodge the flying balls.

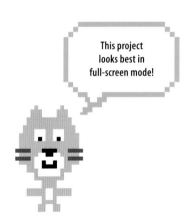

This project looks best in full-screen mode!

▷ **Color control**
You could make a new variable, "PenChange", with its own slider (as in step 10) to control how quickly the lines change color. Insert the new variable block in the "change pen color" block.

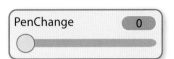

PenChange   0

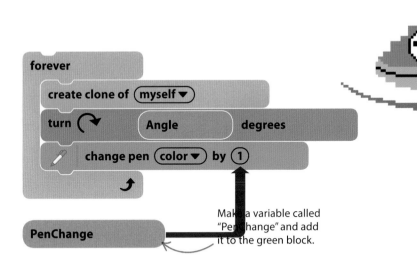

Make a variable called "PenChange" and add it to the green block.

When you find a great spiral, copy the numbers from the sliders to make your preset code.

▷ **Favorites**
You can create keyboard shortcuts to set the spiral's variables to your favorite patterns. Then simply hit the keyboard shortcut to show someone your most dramatic creations.

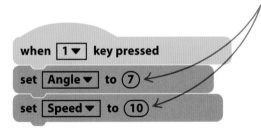

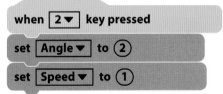

▽ Turn it into art

Add these code blocks to hide the balls and sliders when you press the down arrow key and bring them back with the up arrow key. You can save the picture as an image file on your computer by right-clicking on the stage.

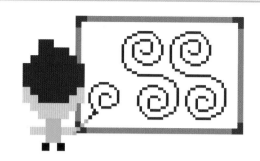

```
when down arrow ▼ key pressed
hide
hide variable Angle ▼
hide variable Speed ▼
```

This block hides all the clones.

These hide the sliders.

```
when up arrow ▼ key pressed
show
show variable Angle ▼
show variable Speed ▼
```

Remember that these code blocks run for all the clones on the stage.

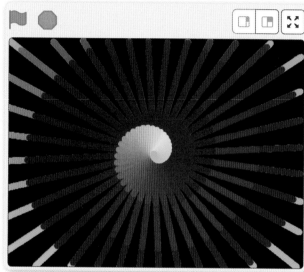

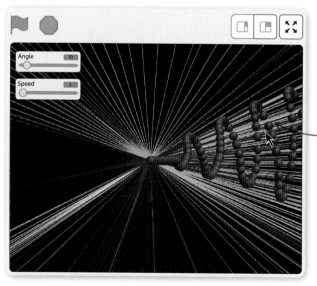

◁ Ball control

Instead of generating clones in a spiral pattern, you can make them follow the mouse-pointer. Just replace the "turn" block with a "point towards mouse-pointer" block. Now try painting with the mouse.

Clones shoot out from the center toward the mouse-pointer.

```
turn ↻ ( Angle ) degrees
```
✗

```
point towards (mouse-pointer ▼)
```
✓

▷ **Sunset**

You can drag the original ball sprite anywhere on the stage and then hit the space bar to clear the old pattern. See if you can create the artificial sunset pattern shown here. Hint: you'll need a pen size of 1 and the "Angle" variable set to 7. Don't forget there's a "go to" block in the code that will reset the position each time the project is run—you can take that block out or change the coordinates once you've found a good sun position. You could even add another full-sized ball sprite in yellow to be the sun.

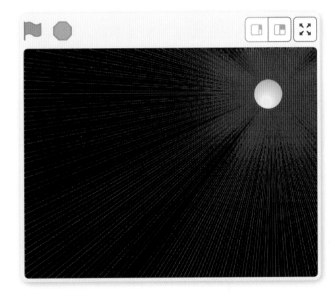

■ ■ **TRY THIS**

Clone lab

Experiment with clones to get a feel for how they work. Start a new project and add a clone creation loop to the cat, and then give each clone a simple bit of code to run when it starts. Experiment with a "pen down" block, or put random numbers in a "go to x: y:" block to see some crazy effects. You can even add some keyboard controls and sound effects for fun. Once you've mastered clones, you'll find you can do all sorts of things in Scratch that are almost impossible without them.

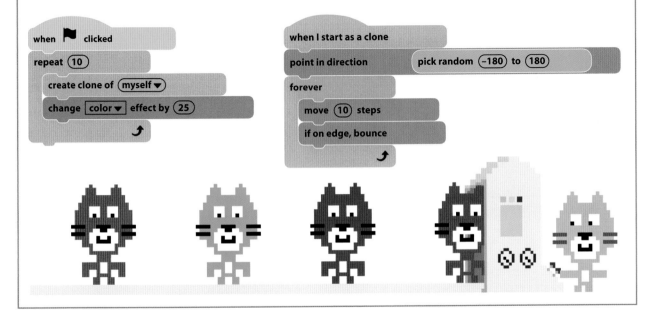

Fantastic Flowers

Create a virtual meadow, and fill it with colorful flowers. In this project, you'll learn how to make your own customized Scratch blocks. Each time one of these runs, it triggers special code called a subprogram, which paints a flower.

Click the green flag to start the project.

How it works

When you run the project, a flower appears wherever you click the mouse. Scratch uses a simple ball sprite and a "stamp" block to draw each flower. The ball stamps an image of itself to create each petal, moving back and forth from the flower's center each time.

draw flower

△ **Subprograms**
Scratch lets you create your own custom blocks to trigger code that you've already built. Then, instead of having to make that code every time you need it, you simply use the new block. Programmers use this trick all the time and call the reused code a subprogram.

draw flower with ④ petals

△ **Adding inputs**
You can create blocks that have windows for inputting numbers or other information, like the example shown here, which lets you set the number of petals.

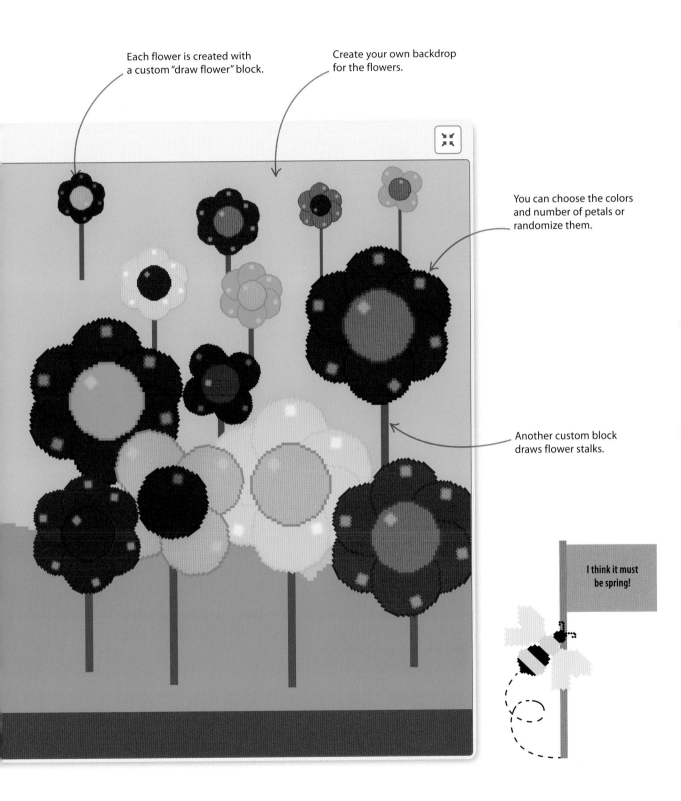

Each flower is created with a custom "draw flower" block.

Create your own backdrop for the flowers.

You can choose the colors and number of petals or randomize them.

Another custom block draws flower stalks.

I think it must be spring!

Make a flower

Follow these steps to make a code that creates a flower when you click on the stage. Once it's working, you can reuse the code to make the special flower-drawing block.

1 Start a new project. Remove the cat sprite by right-clicking on it and selecting "delete". Click on the sprite symbol 🐱 and load the ball sprite from the sprites library. The ball is the building block for making each flower.

Ball

2 Build and run this code to draw a simple flower with five petals. The loop runs five times, drawing a ring of petals centered on the ball sprite's starting position. Each petal is a "stamp" image of the ball sprite. Remember: you'll need to add the Pen extension using the "Add Extension" button at the bottom left.

```
when 🏳 clicked
repeat (5)
    move (25) steps
    stamp
    move (-25) steps
    turn ↻ (360) / (5) degrees
    ↪
stamp
```

The ball moves in the current direction a little and stamps a copy of itself.

It moves back to the center.

It then turns to face a new direction. There are 360 degrees in a full circle, so each turn is one-fifth of a circle.

The "repeat" loop stamps five petals.

The "stamp" block after the loop makes the flower's center.

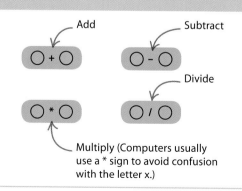

Doing math

Computers are very good at math. You can use the green Operators blocks in Scratch to do simple addition problems. For more complex calculations, you can put Operators blocks inside each other or combine them with other blocks. If blocks are put inside each other, the computer works from the innermost blocks outward, as if the inner blocks were in parentheses.

Add
```
○ + ○
```

Subtract
```
○ - ○
```

```
○ * ○
```

Divide
```
○ / ○
```

Multiply (Computers usually use a * sign to avoid confusion with the letter x.)

More blocks

The next step is to turn the flower-drawing code into a flower-drawing block. You can then use this block to grow flowers wherever you want.

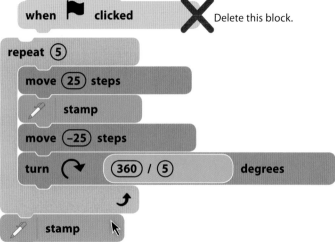

Type the name of the new block here.

3 To make a new Scratch block, select My Blocks in the blocks palette and click "Make a Block". A window will open up. Type in the name of your new block: "draw flower".

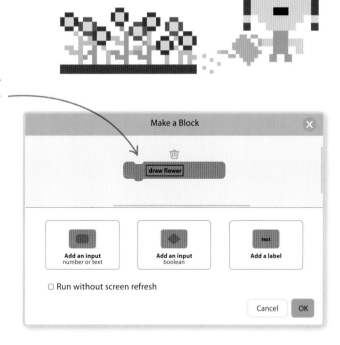

My Blocks

Make a Block

Click here to create the new block.

4 Once you've clicked "OK", you'll see the new block under My Blocks. Before you can use it, you'll need to create the code it will trigger (or "call," as programmers say).

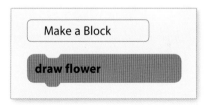

Make a Block

draw flower

5 In the code area, you'll see a new "define" header block with the same name as the block you've just created. Move the flower code under this header. The code will now run whenever the "draw flower" block runs.

when ⚑ clicked ✕ Delete this block.

repeat (5)
move (25) steps
stamp
move (−25) steps
turn ↻ (360) / (5) degrees
↻
stamp

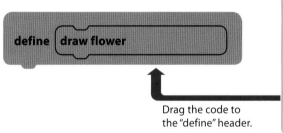

define draw flower

Drag the code to the "define" header.

6 Next, build a new code to use the "draw flower" block. When you run it, you can draw flowers with a click of your mouse.

7 Run the project and click around the stage to create a patch of flowers.

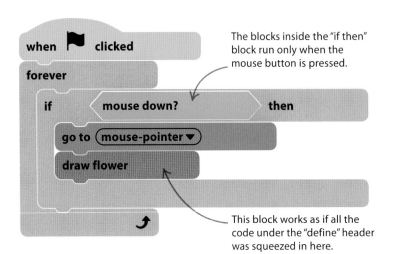

The blocks inside the "if then" block run only when the mouse button is pressed.

This block works as if all the code under the "define" header was squeezed in here.

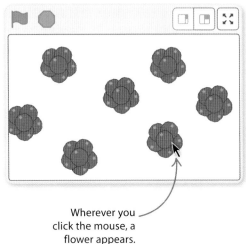

Wherever you click the mouse, a flower appears.

8 The stage will soon fill up, so make some code that clears away the flowers when you press the space bar.

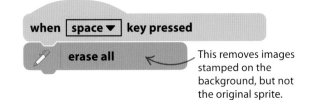

This removes images stamped on the background, but not the original sprite.

Subprograms

Good computer programmers always break up their programs into easily understandable chunks. Code that does something useful that you want to reuse within the program is moved into a "subprogram" and given a name. When the main code runs, or "calls," a subprogram, it's as if the code in the subprogram is inserted at that point. Using subprograms makes programs shorter, easier to understand, and simpler to change. Always give your custom blocks helpful names that describe what they do.

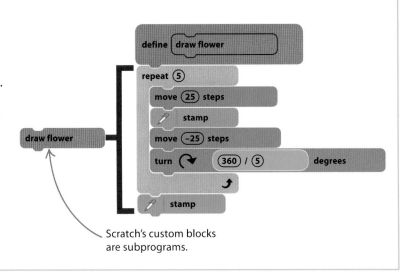

Scratch's custom blocks are subprograms.

Paint by numbers

If you wanted to make a lot of identical flowers, you could simply draw a flower sprite. The real power of custom blocks comes when you add inputs to them to change what they do. To make flowers of different colors with different numbers of petals, you can add input windows to the "draw flower" block.

9 To add an input window to control the number of petals in flowers, right-click (or control/shift-click) on the "define" header block and choose "Edit".

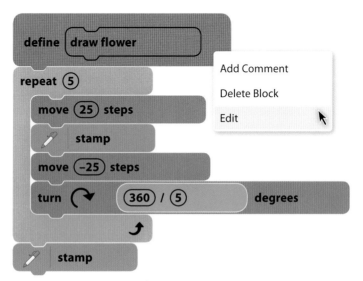

10 A window will open up. Select "Add an input number or text."

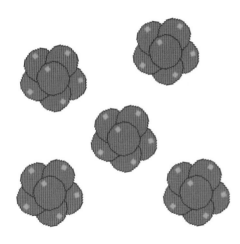

Choose this option.

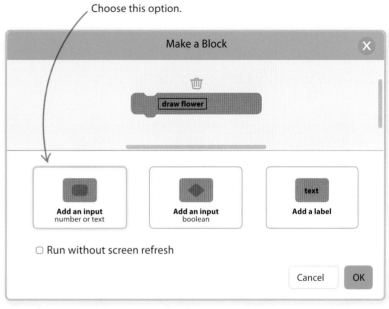

11 An input window now appears in the block. Type "number of petals" into this window and click "OK".

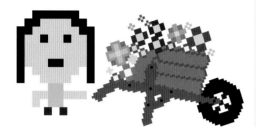

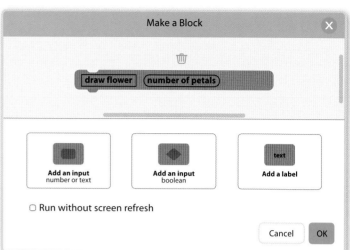

Make a Block

draw flower number of petals

Add an input
number or text

Add an input
boolean

text
Add a label

○ Run without screen refresh

Cancel   OK

12 You'll now see a "number of petals" block in the header block. You can drag copies of this off the header block and drop them into the code. Drag and drop copies into the "repeat" and "turn" blocks where the number of petals (5) is mentioned.

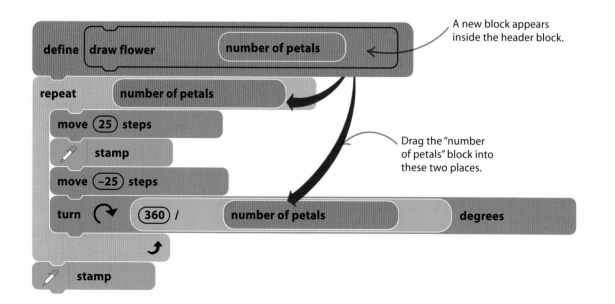

A new block appears inside the header block.

define | draw flower   number of petals

repeat   number of petals

move (25) steps

stamp

move (-25) steps

turn ↻ (360) / number of petals   degrees

stamp

Drag the "number of petals" block into these two places.

13 Look at the "draw flower" block in your code, and you'll see that an input window has appeared. The number you type here will be used in the define code wherever "number of petals" appears. Type in the number seven.

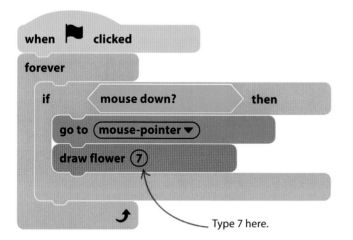

Type 7 here.

14 Run the project and click on the stage. Your flowers should have seven petals. Don't forget—you can clear the stage by pressing the space bar.

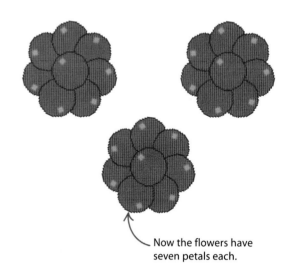

Now the flowers have seven petals each.

15 For more variety, insert a "pick random" block into the "draw flower" block instead of typing in the number of petals. Try it again.

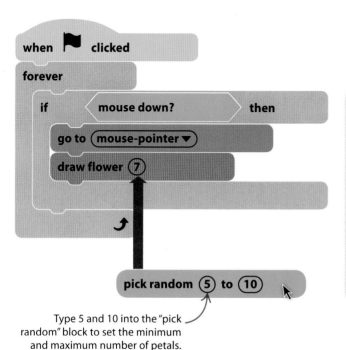

Type 5 and 10 into the "pick random" block to set the minimum and maximum number of petals.

16 Now add extra inputs to change the color of the petals and the flower's center. Right-click on the "define" block again, choose "Edit", and then add two number inputs called "petal color" and "center color".

Click here if you want to delete an input window.

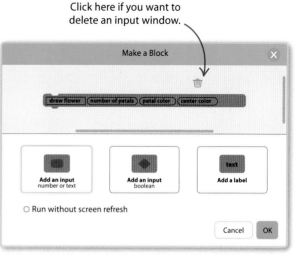

17 Add two new blocks to set the petal and flower-center colors. Remember to drag the correct blocks onto these from the header.

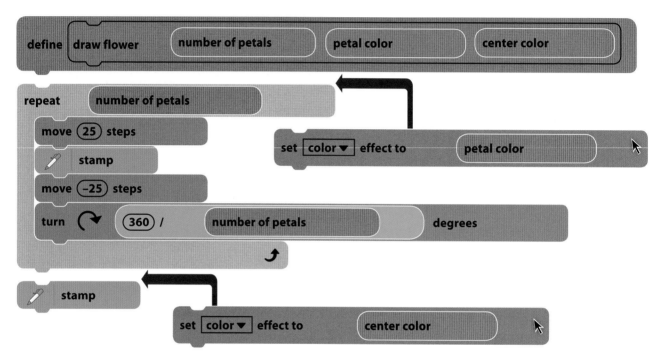

```
define draw flower ( number of petals ) ( petal color ) ( center color )

repeat ( number of petals )
    move (25) steps
    stamp
    move (-25) steps
    turn ↻ ( (360) / ( number of petals ) ) degrees

set [color ▼] effect to ( petal color )

stamp

set [color ▼] effect to ( center color )
```

18 Now add an "erase all" block to the main code. Remove the "pick random" block from the "draw flower" block, and type the numbers 6, 70, and 100 into it to make six-petaled blue flowers. Run the project to make sure it works.

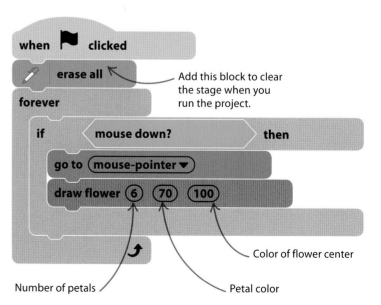

```
when ⚑ clicked
erase all          Add this block to clear
forever            the stage when you
                   run the project.
    if < mouse down? > then
        go to ( mouse-pointer ▼ )
        draw flower (6) (70) (100)
```

Color of flower center

Number of petals   Petal color

19 You can make all your flowers different by using random numbers for each input in the "draw flower" block.

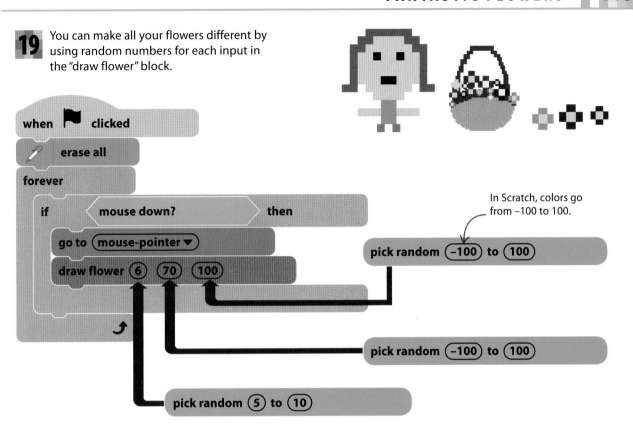

when 🏳 clicked

✏ erase all

forever

if ⟨ mouse down? ⟩ then

go to (mouse-pointer ▼)

draw flower (6) (70) (100)

In Scratch, colors go from –100 to 100.

pick random (–100) to (100)

pick random (–100) to (100)

pick random (5) to (10)

20 Run the project, and click around the stage to make a flower garden. Don't forget you can press the space bar to clear the stage.

Don't forget to save your work from time to time if you use Scratch offline!

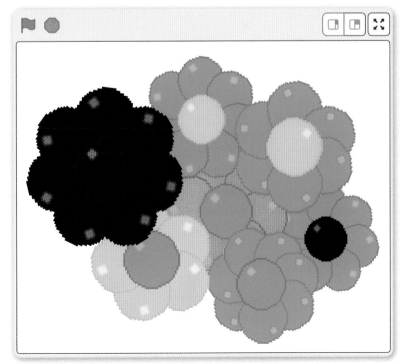

Flower stalks

Real flowers grow on stalks, so follow the next few steps to add stalks to your virtual flowers to make them look more realistic. Using custom blocks makes the code easy to read so you always know what's going on.

21 Choose My Blocks in the blocks palette, and then click "Make a Block". Call the new block "draw stalk". After you've typed the name of the block, add number inputs for the length and thickness of the stalk. Then click "OK".

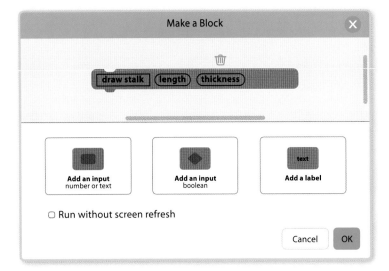

22 Build this code below the "define" header block. Drag the "length" and "thickness" blocks from the header to where they're used in the code.

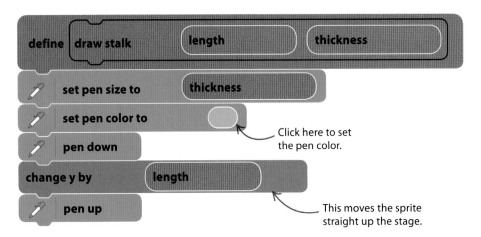

Click here to set the pen color.

This moves the sprite straight up the stage.

23 Next, add the new "draw stalk" block to the main code. Fill in the numbers to set the stalk's length to 100 and its thickness to 5.

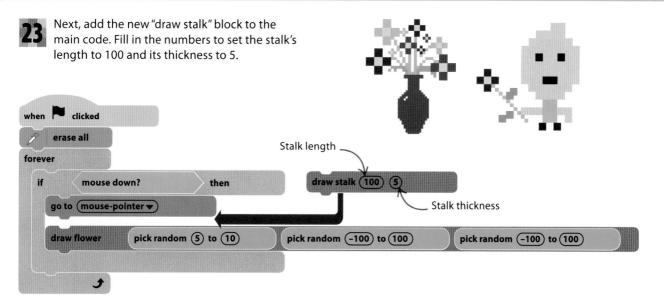

Stalk length

Stalk thickness

24 Run the project. You can now make a whole meadow of colored flowers. Experiment with different numbers in the "pick random" blocks to change the look of your flowers.

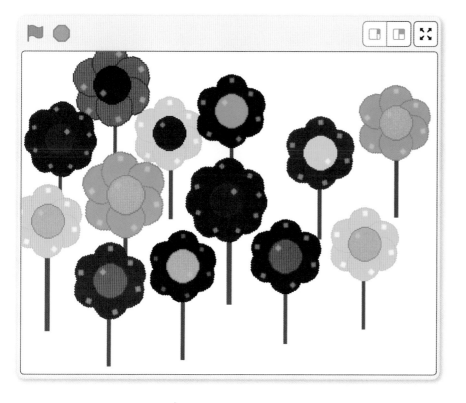

25 For a finishing touch, add a backdrop for your flower meadow. You can paint your own backdrop by clicking the paint symbol ✔ in the backdrops menu to the right of the sprites list. Alternatively, click the backdrop symbol ◪ to load one from the library.

Hacks and tweaks

Feel free to experiment with the code to change the color, size, and shape of the flowers as much as you want. You don't have to use the ball sprite as the template—try creating your own templates to generate more interesting shapes. With a little imagination, you can create all sorts of beautiful scenes.

Give your petal a colored outline if you like.

▷ **Different petals**
Why not use the costume editor to add a different petal to the flowers? Click on the Costumes tab, and add a new costume with the paint symbol ✏. Oval petals work well. You'll need to add blocks to the "define draw flower" code to swap between the petal costume and the ball-a costume for the flower's center.

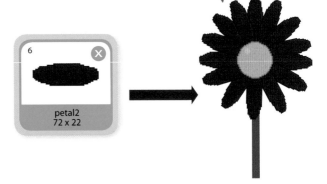

▽ **Flowers everywhere**
Try swapping the main code for this one. It draws flowers in random places automatically, eventually covering the stage with them. Think about how you could add position inputs to the "draw flower" block—you'd need to add x and y inputs and add a "go to" block at the start of the block's definition.

The chosen ranges keep the flowers away from the edges.

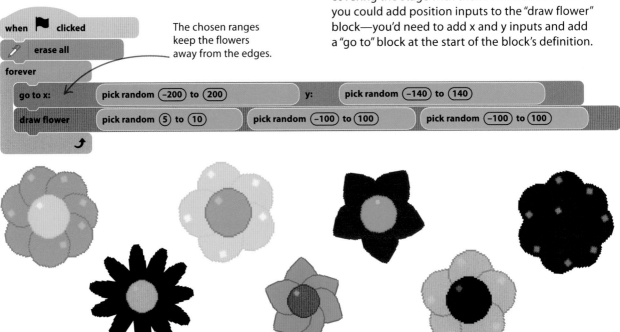

Different sizes

By adding another input to the "draw flower" block, you can control the size of your flowers. You can also make the meadow look more 3-D by making the flowers smaller if they're near the top of the stage, as though farther away.

1 Right-click the "define" header to edit it and add a new input called "scale". Make the changes shown below to the code. When scale is set to 100 in the "draw flower" block, the flowers are drawn at their usual size. Smaller numbers will produce smaller flowers.

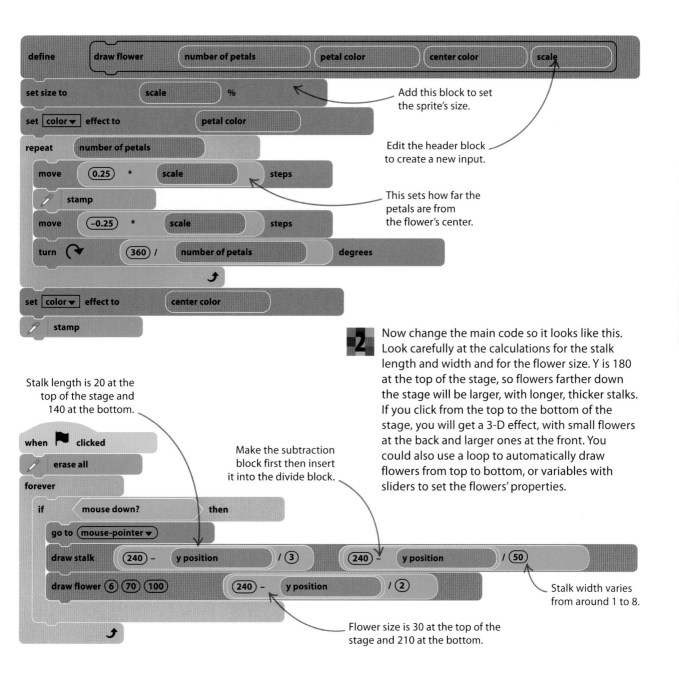

Add this block to set the sprite's size.

Edit the header block to create a new input.

This sets how far the petals are from the flower's center.

Stalk length is 20 at the top of the stage and 140 at the bottom.

Make the subtraction block first then insert it into the divide block.

2 Now change the main code so it looks like this. Look carefully at the calculations for the stalk length and width and for the flower size. Y is 180 at the top of the stage, so flowers farther down the stage will be larger, with longer, thicker stalks. If you click from the top to the bottom of the stage, you will get a 3-D effect, with small flowers at the back and larger ones at the front. You could also use a loop to automatically draw flowers from top to bottom, or variables with sliders to set the flowers' properties.

Stalk width varies from around 1 to 8.

Flower size is 30 at the top of the stage and 210 at the bottom.

Games

Tunnel of Doom

Scratch is the ideal playground for making and perfecting games. To win at this game, you need a steady hand and nerves of steel. Take the cat all the way through the Tunnel of Doom, but don't touch the walls! For an extra challenge, try to beat the best time.

The cat starts here.

How it works

Use your mouse to move the cat all the way through the tunnel without touching the walls. If you accidentally touch a wall, you go back to the start. You can try as many times as you like, but the clock will keep counting the seconds until you finish.

◁ **Cat sprite**
Once the mouse-pointer has touched the cat, the cat follows it everywhere. You don't need to use the mouse button.

◁ **Tunnel**
The tunnel maze is a giant sprite that fills the stage. The tunnel itself isn't actually part of the sprite—it's a gap that you create by using the eraser tool in Scratch's paint editor. If the cat stays in the middle of the path, it won't be detected as touching the tunnel sprite.

◁ **Home**
When the cat touches the home sprite, the game ends with a celebration.

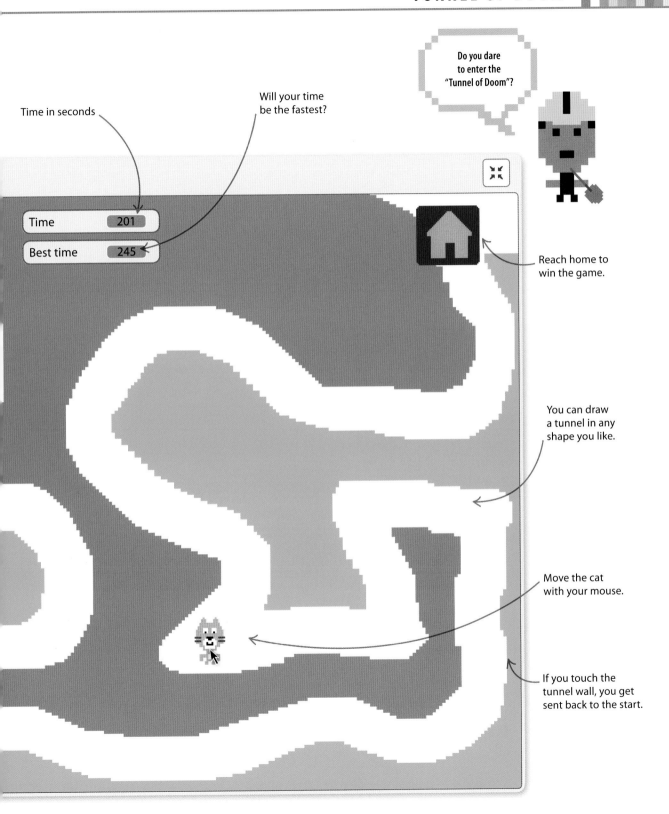

Do you dare to enter the "Tunnel of Doom"?

Time in seconds

Will your time be the fastest?

Time 201

Best time 245

Reach home to win the game.

You can draw a tunnel in any shape you like.

Move the cat with your mouse.

If you touch the tunnel wall, you get sent back to the start.

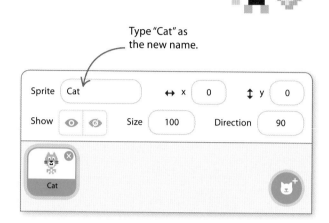

Set the mood

Start by setting the scene for the game with some appropriate music. You can choose any music you like from the sound library in Scratch by following the steps below.

1 Start a new project. Let the cat sprite stay, but change its name from Sprite1 to Cat to keep things simple.

Type "Cat" as the new name.

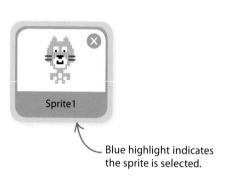

Blue highlight indicates the sprite is selected.

| Sprite | Cat | | ↔ x | 0 | ↕ y | 0 |
| Show | 👁 👁 | Size | 100 | | Direction | 90 |

Cat

2 Before building any code, add some music to create the right atmosphere for the game. Click on the Sounds tab above the blocks palette and then on the speaker symbol ◀» to open the sound library. Now choose "Drive Around". To preview a sound, click the play symbol.

Click here to preview a sound.

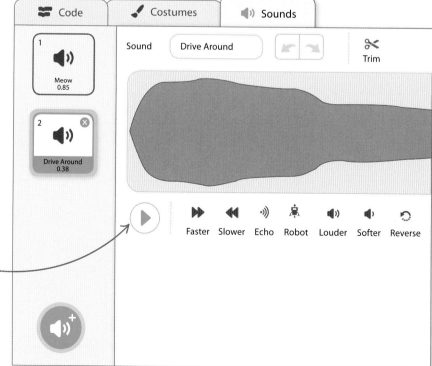

3 Add this code to the cat sprite to loop the music. Use the "play sound until done" block, not "start sound"; otherwise, things go wrong as Scratch tries to play your sound lots of times at once.

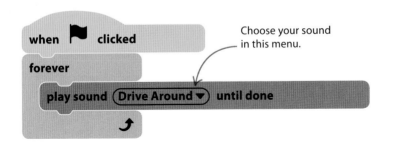

Choose your sound in this menu.

```
when [flag] clicked
forever
    play sound (Drive Around ▼) until done
```

4 Now run the project, and the music should play ... forever. Click on the red stop button above the stage to stop it again.

Creating the tunnel

The next step is to make the twisted tunnel that will challenge the player's nerve and steadiness of hand. How you draw the tunnel affects the difficulty of the game.

5 Click the paint symbol ✔ in the sprites menu to create a new sprite with the paint editor. Choose a color you like, and click on the fill tool ♦. Then click anywhere in the paint area to fill it with a solid color.

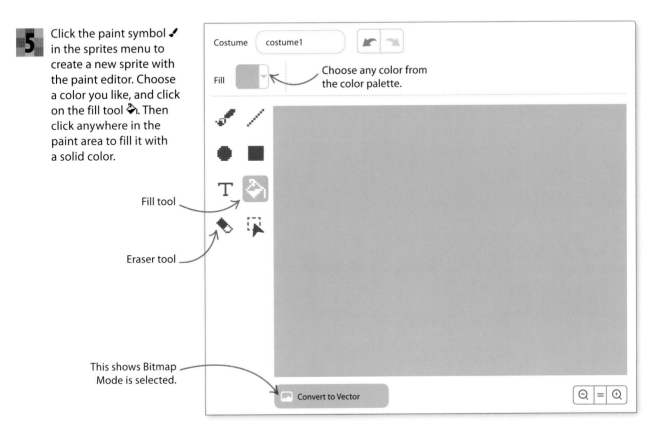

Choose any color from the color palette.

Fill tool

Eraser tool

This shows Bitmap Mode is selected.

6 Now select the eraser tool, and use the spinner buttons next to its icon at the top of the painting area to set the width of the tunnel.

Eraser tool

7 Use the eraser to make gaps in the top left and top right where the maze starts and ends. Then draw a wiggly tunnel between the two corners. If things go wrong, click the undo symbol ↰ at the top and try again.

Make sure the eraser is nearly full size.

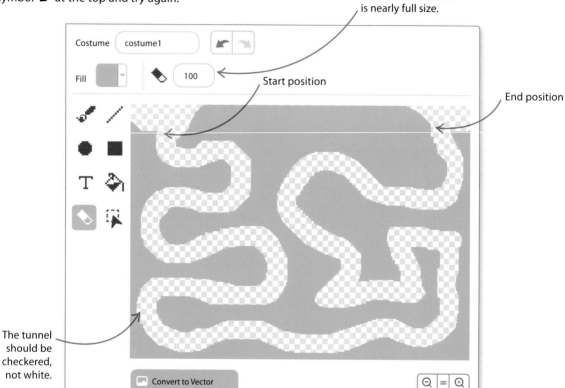

Start position

End position

The tunnel should be checkered, not white.

8 To make the maze look more interesting, use the fill tool to paint the central area a different color. Don't fill the tunnel with a color, or the game won't work.

Click in this area to fill it with a second color.

9 Now click on this sprite in the sprites list and rename it "Tunnel".

Tunnel

10 With the tunnel sprite selected in the sprites list, click on the Code tab and build this code to position it correctly and to animate it. Run the project to test it.

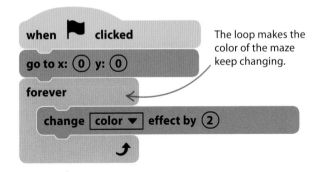

when 🏴 clicked

go to x: (0) y: (0)

forever

change [color ▼] effect by (2)

The loop makes the color of the maze keep changing.

Mouse control

Now add some code to the cat to turn the project into a working game. The code blocks build step by step, so test them as you go along to make sure they work properly.

11 Select the cat sprite, and add this code. It shrinks the cat and positions it at the start of the tunnel. Once the mouse-pointer touches the cat, it will move with the mouse. Note that players don't need to click on the cat to pick it up. The code stops with a "Meow" if the cat touches the tunnel walls.

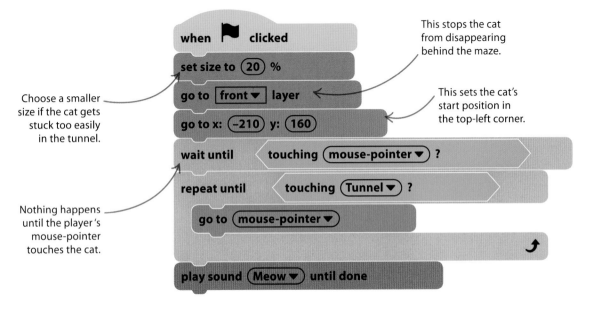

This stops the cat from disappearing behind the maze.

Choose a smaller size if the cat gets stuck too easily in the tunnel.

This sets the cat's start position in the top-left corner.

Nothing happens until the player's mouse-pointer touches the cat.

when 🏴 clicked

set size to (20) %

go to [front ▼] layer

go to x: (-210) y: (160)

wait until < touching (mouse-pointer ▼) ? >

repeat until < touching (Tunnel ▼) ? >

go to (mouse-pointer ▼)

play sound (Meow ▼) until done

Repeat until loops

The useful "repeat until" loop repeats the blocks inside it until the condition at the top of the block becomes true, and then the blocks below are run. The block makes it easier to write simple, readable code, like this example.

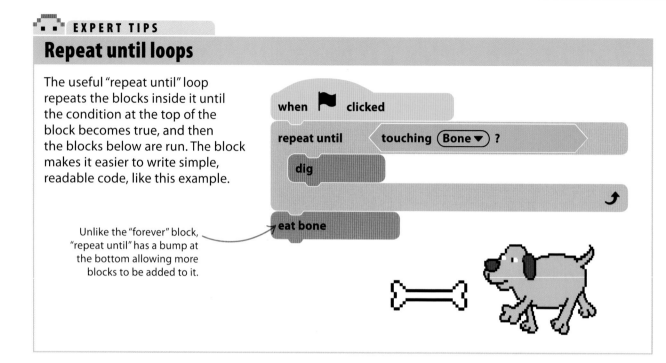

Unlike the "forever" block, "repeat until" has a bump at the bottom allowing more blocks to be added to it.

12 Run the game. You should be able to control the cat once you've touched it with your mouse-pointer. Try moving it along the tunnel. If you touch the wall, the cat will meow and get stuck. If the cat gets stuck too often, reduce the number in the "set size" block, but don't make it too easy.

Help, I'm stuck!

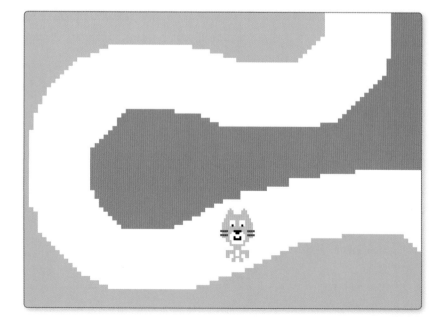

13 At the moment, you have to restart the game if you touch the wall. Add this loop to the code to send the cat back to the start for another try if it touches the wall. Test the game again.

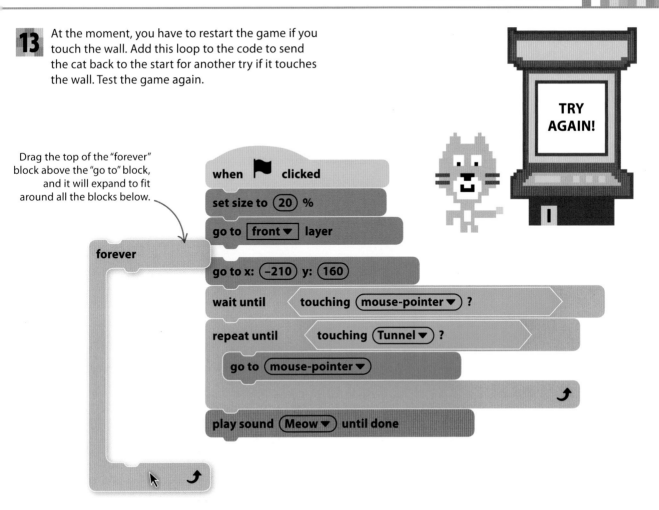

Drag the top of the "forever" block above the "go to" block, and it will expand to fit around all the blocks below.

TRY AGAIN!

14 Click the sprite symbol 🐱 in the sprites list to add a new sprite to the game. Choose the Home Button sprite and rename it "Home" in the sprites list. On the stage, drag it into the top-right corner.

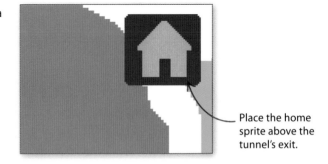

Place the home sprite above the tunnel's exit.

15 It will probably be too big, so add this code to shrink it. Run the project, and reposition the house on the stage if you need to.

16 Next, you need to add some code to check whether the cat has made it home. Select the cat in the sprites list, and add the blocks shown here. The blocks inside the "if then" block run only if the cat is touching the house.

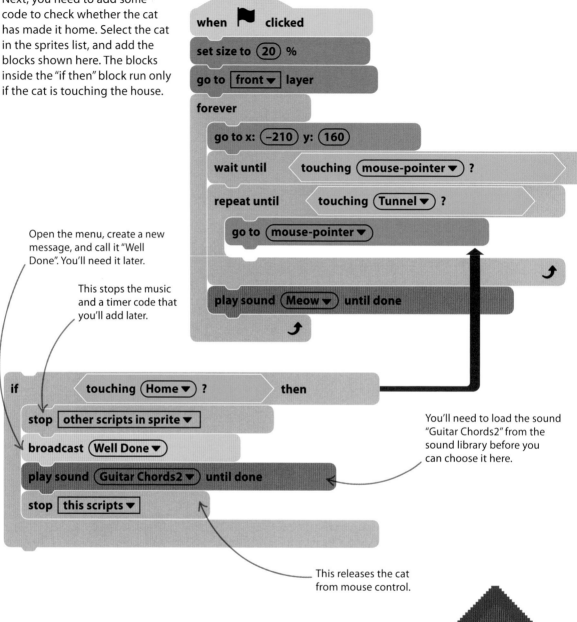

when ⚑ clicked

set size to (20) %

go to front ▼ layer

forever

go to x: (−210) y: (160)

wait until ⟨ touching (mouse-pointer ▼) ? ⟩

repeat until ⟨ touching (Tunnel ▼) ? ⟩

go to (mouse-pointer ▼)

play sound (Meow ▼) until done

Open the menu, create a new message, and call it "Well Done". You'll need it later.

This stops the music and a timer code that you'll add later.

if ⟨ touching (Home ▼) ? ⟩ then

stop [other scripts in sprite ▼]

broadcast (Well Done ▼)

play sound (Guitar Chords2 ▼) until done

stop [this scripts ▼]

You'll need to load the sound "Guitar Chords2" from the sound library before you can choose it here.

This releases the cat from mouse control.

17 Run the game again. Try getting through the tunnel to the house. When you succeed, the music should stop, the cat will stop moving, and your celebration music will play. If you can't get through the tunnels, then you need to make the cat smaller, but you can test the game's end by clicking on the cat and dragging it home (this is cheating!).

Against the clock

Tunnel of Doom is more fun if you add a timer to show how quickly you've made it through the tunnel. Then you can challenge other players to beat your best time.

18 Click on Variables in the blocks palette, and make a variable called "Time". Leave the check box checked so the variable is shown on the stage.

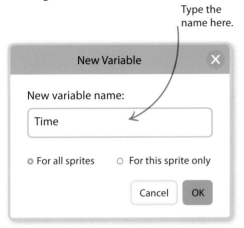

Type the name here.

19 Add this code to the cat. It simply counts the seconds since the game started. Move the "Time" variable to the top center of the stage so the player can see it easily.

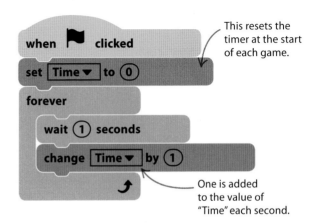

This resets the timer at the start of each game.

One is added to the value of "Time" each second.

20 Try the game again. When you get the cat home, the timer stops, leaving your final time displayed on the stage.

Wow! That was a speedy escape.

21 To make winning the game feel more rewarding, add a new sprite to show a message congratulating the player. Click on the paint symbol ✎ to make a sign in the paint editor using colored shapes and the text tool. The one shown here is just a suggestion—you can use your own ideas.

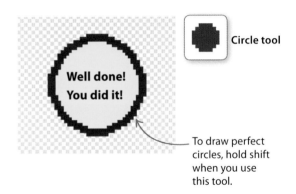

Circle tool

To draw perfect circles, hold shift when you use this tool.

22 To make the sign work, add these code blocks to your new sprite. The first one hides the sign when the project starts, and the second is triggered when the "Well Done" message is sent by the cat. It displays the sign and makes it flash.

23 Your game is now complete. Test it thoroughly (by playing lots), and then challenge your friends to see if they can beat your times.

```
when 🏳 clicked
hide
go to x: ⓪ y: ⓪
```

The sprite shouldn't be seen at the start of the game.

This puts the sprite in the center of the stage.

```
when I receive  Well Done ▼
show
go to  front ▼  layer
forever
    change  color ▼  effect by  (20)
    ↻
```

Rapid color changes make the sign flash.

Hacks and tweaks

This game is bursting with possibilities. Save a copy and start experimenting! You could add extra sound effects or extra sprites, such as a floating ghost to scare the cat back to the start or a friendly bat that jumps the player to a later spot in the tunnel.

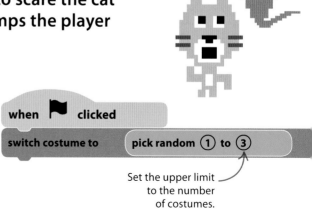

▷ **Let's twist again**
You can make the game harder or easier by changing how wide and twisted the tunnel is. You could also create tunnels with branches—perhaps make the player choose between a short narrow tunnel and a long wide one. You could even make several different costumes for the tunnel sprite and choose a random one at the start of each game by adding this code.

```
when 🏳 clicked
switch costume to    pick random ① to ③
```

Set the upper limit to the number of costumes.

▽ Best time

You can make the game show the best time achieved
so far, like a high score. Make a new variable called
"Best time" and drag it next to the "Time" display
on the stage. Then add the code below to the cat
to capture new best times when the cat gets home.

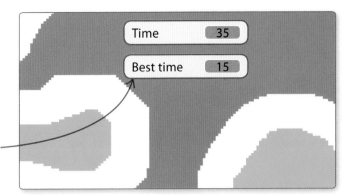

Time　　35

Best time　　15

The best time
achieved is shown
on the stage.

This block is true
the first time you
run the game.

True if your time
was quicker than
the old record.

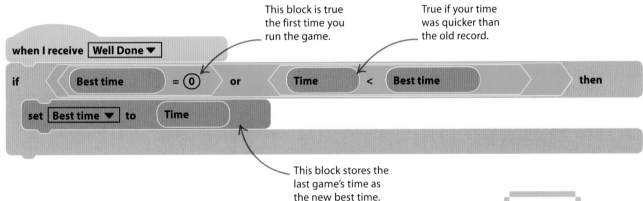

```
when I receive  Well Done ▼

if       Best time       = 0    or     Time    <    Best time          then

    set  Best time ▼  to    Time
```

This block stores the
last game's time as
the new best time.

▽ Who's the best?

You can display the name of the quickest player by
making another variable, "Best player", and showing
it on the stage. Add these two blocks shown here to
the best-time code.

I won!
Let's celebrate!

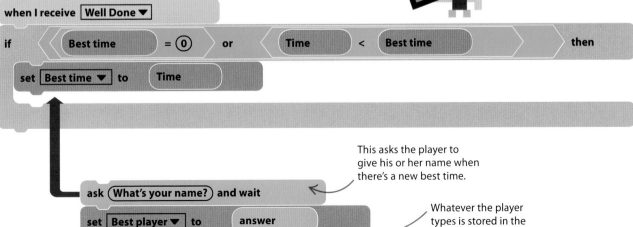

```
when I receive  Well Done ▼

if       Best time       = 0    or     Time    <    Best time          then

    set  Best time ▼  to    Time

        ask  What's your name?  and wait

        set  Best player ▼  to        answer
```

This asks the player to
give his or her name when
there's a new best time.

Whatever the player
types is stored in the
"answer" block once.

Window Cleaner

Messy windows? You'd better get up and clean them! This frantic game counts how many splats you can clean off your computer screen in a minute. You can wipe away the splats either by using a computer mouse or by waving your hand in front of a webcam.

How it works

The game starts by cloning a splat sprite and scattering clones with different costumes randomly across the stage. When motion is detected by the webcam, Scratch uses its "ghost" effect to make the splats fade. If you wave your hand enough, they eventually disappear. The aim of the game is to remove as many splats as you can in one minute.

▽ **Splat sprite**
This game has one sprite with several costumes, which you'll paint yourself. By cloning the sprite, you can cover the screen with splats of messy gunk.

Each splat is a clone of the project's single sprite.

Wave your hand to rub out the splats.

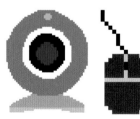

△ **Controls**
First, you'll clean up the splats with your mouse, but later you can change the code to detect the movement of your hand with a webcam.

Slime time!

To make some mess on the screen, you need to draw some slimy splats. Follow these instructions, and you'll be in a mess in no time at all.

1 Start a new project. Remove the cat sprite by right-clicking (or control/shift-clicking) on it and selecting "delete". Click on the paint symbol ✔ in the sprites menu to paint a new sprite.

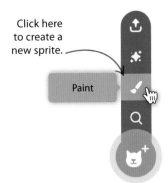

Click here to create a new sprite.

Paint

2 The paint editor will open. Click on "Convert to Bitmap". To make your first splat, choose a color from the palette.

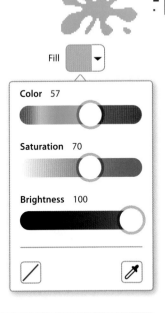

Fill

Color   57

Saturation   70

Brightness   100

3 Select the brush tool and draw the outline of a large splat. Use the entire painting area since the splat will get shrunk later.

Brush tool

Yay! This is more fun than paintball!

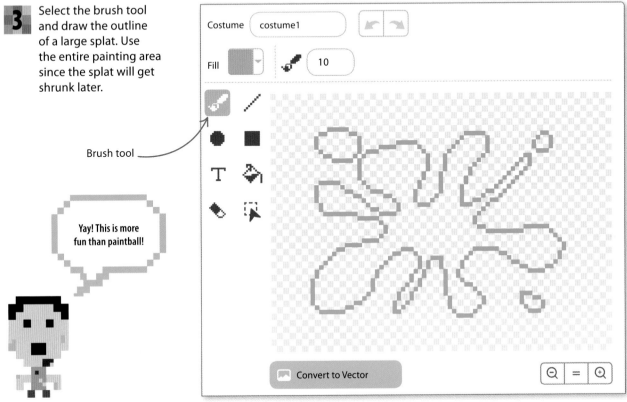

Costume   costume1

Fill

10

Convert to Vector

4 Next, choose the fill tool and click inside the outline to make a solid splat.

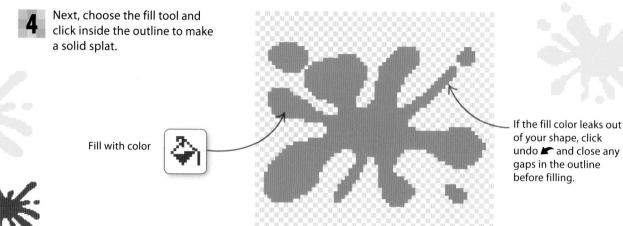

Fill with color

If the fill color leaks out of your shape, click undo ↶ and close any gaps in the outline before filling.

5 To make another splat costume, click on the paint symbol ✏ in the costumes menu at the bottom left (not the one in the sprites list). This will make a new blank costume. Draw a splat with a different color. Make at least four costumes altogether.

Paint

Click here to create new costumes.

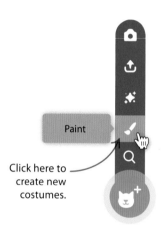

costume1
401 x 304

costume2
384 x 244

Vanishing splats

Now it's time to add code to the splat sprite to make the game work. Follow the next steps to make several clones appear and then disappear when the mouse-pointer touches them.

6 Click on the Code tab to make some variables. Choose Variables in the blocks palette, and then select the "Make a Variable" button to create three variables: "MaxSplats", "Score", and "SplatsOnScreen".

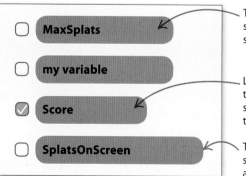

MaxSplats

my variable

Score

SplatsOnScreen

The maximum number of splats that can be on the screen at any one time.

Leave the box checked so the score appears on the stage. Uncheck the other three boxes.

The actual number of splats on the screen at the moment.

7 Add this code to the splat sprite. It sets the maximum number of splats on the screen to 10 and resets the "Score" and "SplatsOnScreen" to 0, ready for a new game. The "forever" loop checks whether there are fewer splats than the maximum and, if so, adds a new one. Don't run the game yet since you won't see anything.

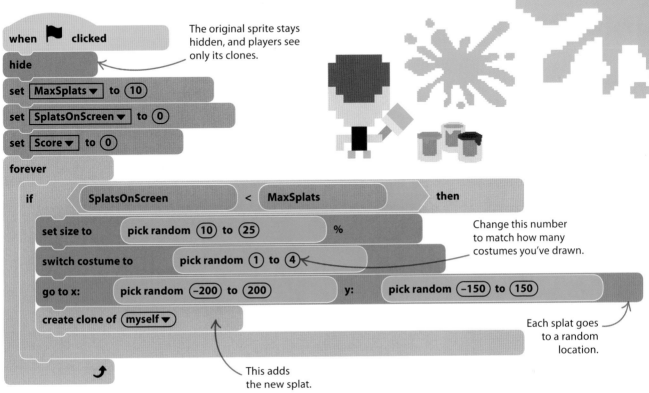

The original sprite stays hidden, and players see only its clones.

```
when [flag] clicked
hide
set [MaxSplats ▼] to (10)
set [SplatsOnScreen ▼] to (0)
set [Score ▼] to (0)
forever
    if < SplatsOnScreen < MaxSplats > then
        set size to (pick random (10) to (25)) %
        switch costume to (pick random (1) to (4))
        go to x: (pick random (-200) to (200)) y: (pick random (-150) to (150))
        create clone of (myself ▼)
```

Change this number to match how many costumes you've drawn.

Each splat goes to a random location.

This adds the new splat.

8 Add this second bit of code to the sprite. Each new clone will run it. It makes the new splat visible (it's hidden at first) and then waits for the mouse-pointer to touch the splat. When it does, the splat disappears with a "pop," and the player scores a point.

The clone is hidden when it's created, so you need to show it.

This keeps track of the number of splats.

```
when I start as a clone
change [SplatsOnScreen ▼] by (1)
show
wait until < touching (mouse-pointer ▼) ? >
change [Score ▼] by (1)
change [SplatsOnScreen ▼] by (-1)
start sound (pop ▼)
delete this clone
```

Nothing happens until the player's mouse-pointer touches the splat.

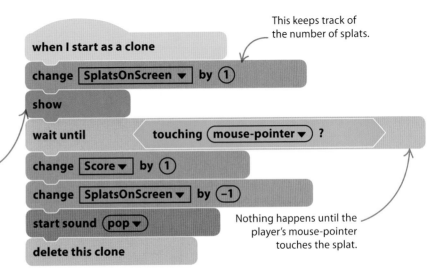
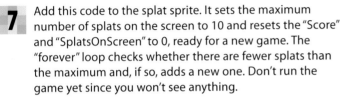

9 Run the game to test it. Ten splats should appear. You should be able to remove the splats by touching them with the mouse-pointer, but new splats will appear, too. However, there's a problem—the game never comes to an end.

Goodbye, splat!

Countdown

Nothing puts players under pressure like a time limit. The next bit of code will give players a one-minute countdown in which to zap as many splats as they can.

10 Make a new variable and call it "Countdown." This will tell players how much time is left. Keep it checked so it appears on the stage.

11 Add this code to launch the countdown. Once the timer has ticked down, it stops the other code blocks from making any more splats and sends out a message that you'll need later on.

Set the number of seconds here.

```
when 🏳 clicked
set Countdown ▼ to 60
repeat until     Countdown          < 1
    wait 1 seconds
    change Countdown ▼ by -1
stop other scripts in sprite ▼
broadcast Time's Up! ▼
```

Tick down a second.

This stops new splats from appearing.

Select "New message" in the menu and call it "Time's Up!"

12 Test the game. It should end when the timer reaches 0. But there's a small problem: any leftover splats can still be cleaned up for points, even though the game's over. To prevent this, add this tiny bit of code to remove any remaining splats. Now try the game again.

```
when I receive Time's Up! ▼
delete this clone
```

Every clone will run this code, so all the clones will be deleted.

Camera control

You can make the window cleaning more realistic by adding camera controls. You'll need a webcam attached to your computer to complete the next section. When playing the game with the webcam, stand well back from the computer screen so that most of your body is visible on the stage.

13 Make a new variable and call it "Difficulty". This can be set anywhere from 0 to 100—the higher the number, the harder the game. Uncheck the check box so the variable isn't shown on the stage.

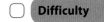

○ **Difficulty**

14 To use the webcam, you need to add the Video Motion extension. Click "Add Extension" at the bottom left of the screen, and then choose Video Motion. The blocks will now be in the section called "Video Motion". Add this code to set the value of "Difficulty" and turn on the webcam. Try setting "Difficulty" to 40 to start with. You can adjust the value later if the lighting and background in your room make the game too easy or too hard. Don't run the game yet.

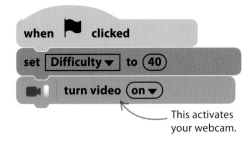

when ⚑ clicked
set Difficulty ▼ to 40
🎥 turn video on ▼

This activates your webcam.

15 To use the camera to delete the splats instead of the mouse, change the "when I start as a clone" code like this.

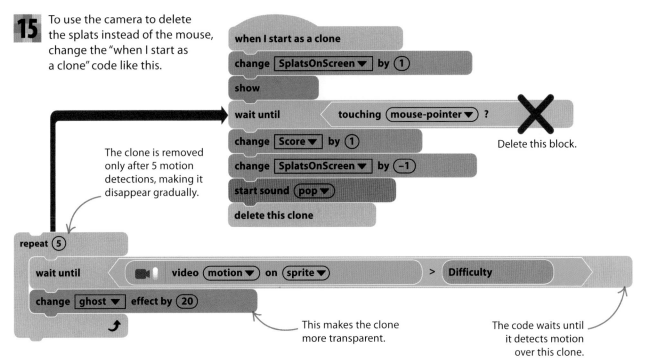

when I start as a clone
change SplatsOnScreen ▼ by 1
show
wait until ⟨ touching mouse-pointer ▼ ? ⟩

Delete this block.

change Score ▼ by 1
change SplatsOnScreen ▼ by -1
start sound pop ▼
delete this clone

The clone is removed only after 5 motion detections, making it disappear gradually.

repeat 5
wait until ⟨ 🎥 video motion ▼ on sprite ▼ > Difficulty ⟩
change ghost ▼ effect by 20

This makes the clone more transparent.

The code waits until it detects motion over this clone.

△ **How it works**
The old code just waited for the mouse-pointer to touch the splat clone before removing it. Now we wait for the webcam to detect motion in the area touching the clone, but we do this five times, increasing the ghost effect each time so the clone gets fainter. So as you rub the splat, it becomes transparent and then disappears.

16 Run the game. You'll probably get a pop-up asking if Scratch can use your webcam. It's okay to click "Accept". You'll then be able to see yourself behind the splats. Try rubbing some splats out with your hand. If they aren't disappearing, put a lower number in the "set Difficulty" block and rerun the game.

Click here to switch to full screen.

It's easier to play this game in full-screen mode.

Hacks and tweaks

Here are some tips to tweak this game, but feel free to try out your own ideas. Once you know how to use Scratch's motion-detection feature, you can create all sorts of games that encourage players to jump around and have fun!

The "High Score" variable changes only when a player beats it.

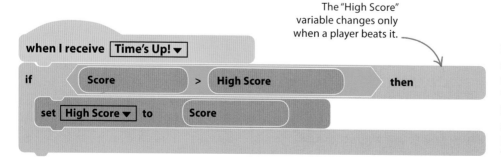

◁ **High score**
It's easy to add a high score to the game: just make a new variable, "High Score", and add this code. You could also show the top player's name (see how in the Tunnel of Doom project).

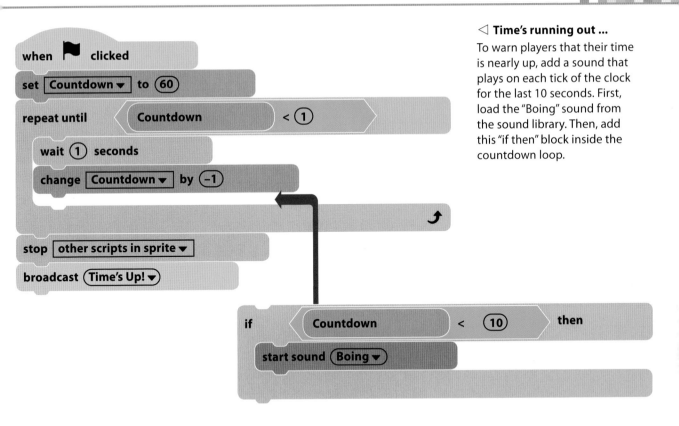

◁ **Time's running out …**
To warn players that their time is nearly up, add a sound that plays on each tick of the clock for the last 10 seconds. First, load the "Boing" sound from the sound library. Then, add this "if then" block inside the countdown loop.

▽ **Difficulty slider**
If you find you have to change the difficulty setting a lot, you can display it on the stage as a slider. Check the variable's check box to make it appear on the stage. Then right-click (or control/shift-click) on it and choose "slider".

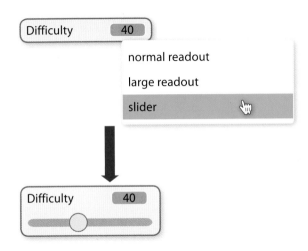

TRY THIS

Multiplayer version

Here's a challenge to test your coding skills. Save a copy of your Window Cleaner game and then try to adapt it to make a multiplayer game in which each player has to rub out splats of a particular color. You'll need to create score variables for each player, and you'll need to add "if then" blocks to the clones' code to update the different scores depending on which costume has been rubbed out.

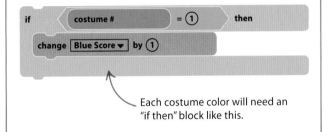

Each costume color will need an "if then" block like this.

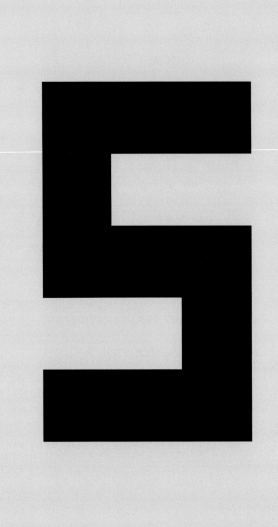

Simulations

Virtual Snow

You don't want real snow inside your computer—
it would melt and ruin the circuits. This project
shows you how to make perfectly safe virtual
snow using Scratch. It falls from the sky and
can be made to settle on the ground or stick
to things.

How it works

Each snowflake is a clone that moves down
the stage from top to bottom, jiggling from side
to side like a real snowflake. When the snowflake
lands on something or hits the bottom, it stamps
an image of itself.

The snowflakes are clones
of a simple circle shape.

Snow falls from the top
and settles at the bottom.

The snow piles
up on the sprite.

△ **Snowman**
In this project, you can load any
sprite and make snow stick to it.
The snowman sprite works well.

△ **Hidden pictures**
You can add invisible objects that
slowly reveal themselves as the
snow sticks to them. Use a sprite
from the library, draw your own
object, or write your name in
huge letters.

Let it snow

Start off by drawing the snowflake costume, which is simply a white circle. Then make it snow by creating clones—each one a tiny snowflake falling from the top to the bottom of the stage.

1 Start a new project. Delete the cat sprite, and click on the paint symbol ✏ in the sprites menu to make a new sprite with the paint editor. Before you start painting, rename the sprite "Snowflake".

Type "Snowflake" here.

Information panel

2 In the paint editor, choose the circle tool and draw a small white circle in the middle. Hold down the shift key as you draw the circle to make sure it isn't oval-shaped.

Choose solid color here.

Circle tool

Select white

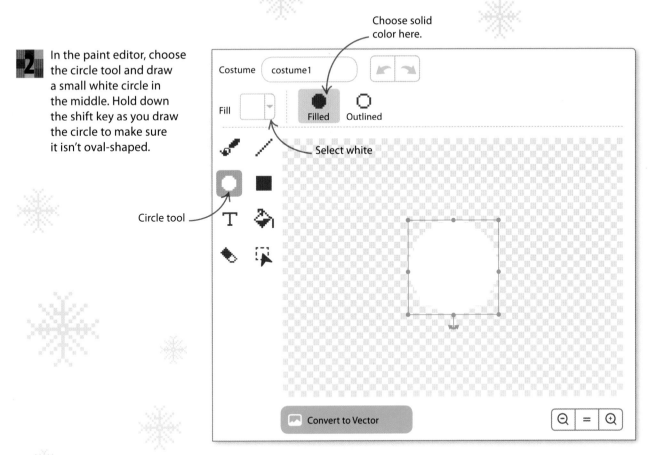

3 To make sure the circle is the right size, drag one of the corners of the box that appears around it to resize the circle. Aim for a size of 50 x 50. If the box disappears, use the select tool to draw it around the circle again.

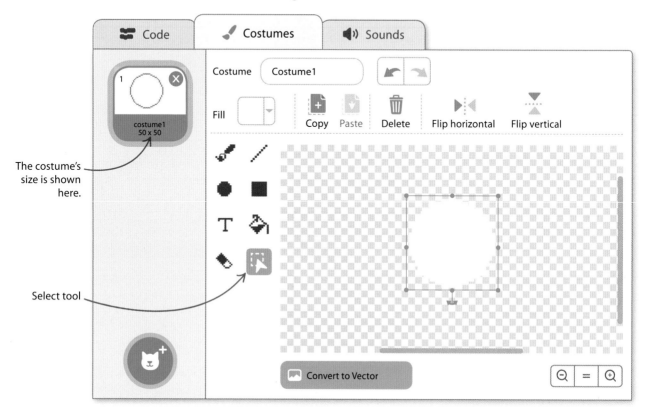

The costume's size is shown here.

Select tool

4 Now add a background so that you can see the falling snow. Click on the paint symbol ✔ in the backdrops menu to create a new backdrop in the paint editor.

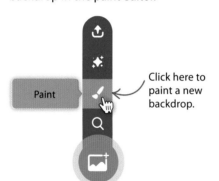

Click here to paint a new backdrop.

Paint

5 To make things more interesting, you can use a blend of two colors to fill the background. Make sure "Convert to Bitmap" is selected in the bottom left. Then select the fill tool and choose the vertical gradient option. Choose the darkest blue as your first stored color and a paler blue as the second stored color.

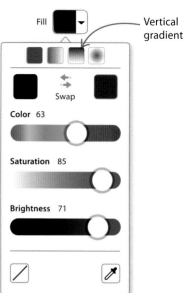

Fill

Vertical gradient

Swap

Color 63

Saturation 85

Brightness 71

6 Now select the fill tool and click in the backdrop to fill it. You can use any colors you like, but snow shows up better on dark colors.

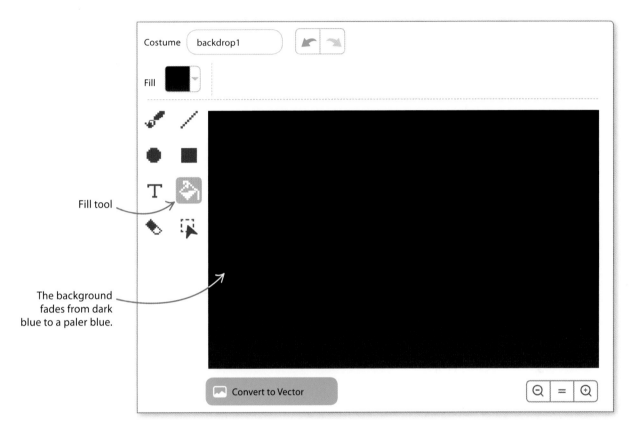

Costume backdrop1

Fill

Fill tool

The background fades from dark blue to a paler blue.

Convert to Vector

7 You'll need to add the Pen extension as you did in previous projects (see page 100). Select the snowflake from the sprites list and open the Code tab. Add this code to make clones of the snowflake. Don't run the project yet.

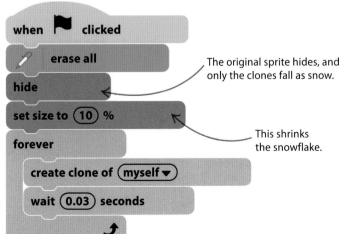

```
when [flag] clicked
    erase all
hide
set size to (10) %
forever
    create clone of (myself ▾)
    wait (0.03) seconds
```

The original sprite hides, and only the clones fall as snow.

This shrinks the snowflake.

8 Now add this code to make the cloned snowflakes fall from the top of the stage to the bottom, jiggling as they go.

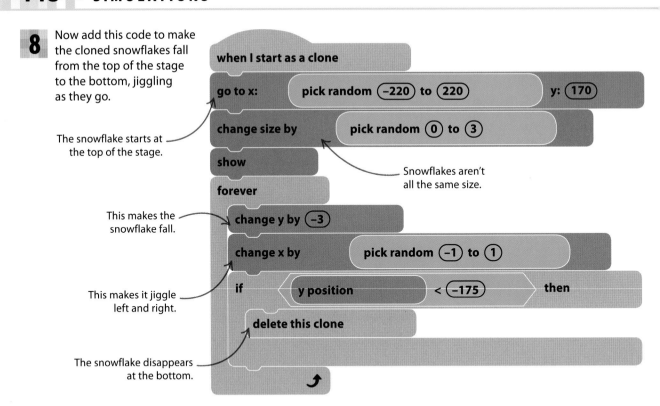

when I start as a clone

go to x: pick random (−220) to (220) y: (170)

The snowflake starts at the top of the stage.

change size by pick random (0) to (3)

show

Snowflakes aren't all the same size.

forever

This makes the snowflake fall.

change y by (−3)

change x by pick random (−1) to (1)

This makes it jiggle left and right.

if < y position < (−175) > then

delete this clone

The snowflake disappears at the bottom.

9 Run the project. The snow should fall down the stage before disappearing at the bottom.

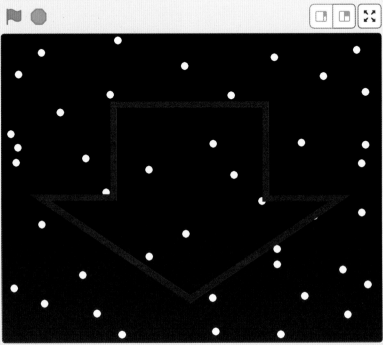

Snowdrifts

In really cold weather, snow doesn't just vanish when it hits the ground—it piles up. It's simple to make your virtual snow settle or stick to other things. Just follow these steps.

10 First to make the snow settle at the bottom. You could just leave the clones there, but Scratch won't let more than 300 clones appear on the stage at once, so you'd run out of snow. An easy fix is to stamp a copy of each clone before deleting it.

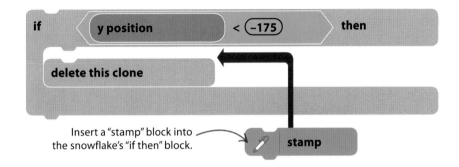

Insert a "stamp" block into the snowflake's "if then" block.

11 Run the project, and snow should collect on the floor, but only in a thin layer. To make it build up, add another "if then" block to stamp copies of the clones whenever they touch anything white—such as other snowflakes.

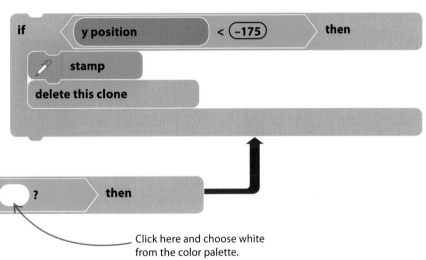

Click here and choose white from the color palette.

12 Run the project and watch the snow pile up. You'll notice a problem. The snowflakes are building up in beautiful sculptures instead of settling in a blanket, as real snow does.

Snowflakes stick to anything white.

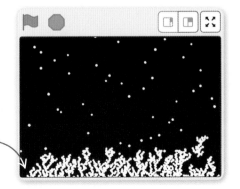

There's no business like snow business!

13 To make the snow settle in a thick blanket, try this change to the code. Now when a snowflake touches something white, it rolls a die—only if it gets a 1 does it stick. This makes the snow less sticky and more likely to travel farther and build a solid layer.

Add an "and" block to make sure both conditions are true.

This block is true when Scratch rolls a 1.

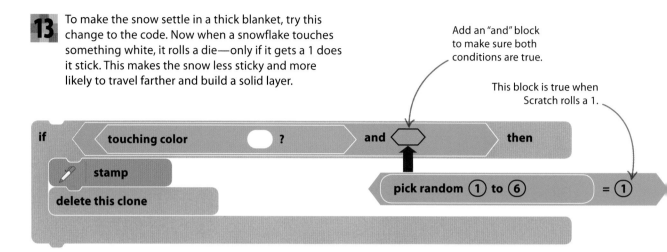

if ⟨ touching color ⬭ ? ⟩ and ⟨ ⟩ then
  🖊 stamp
  delete this clone

pick random ① to ⑥ = ①

14 Run the project to see what happens. You can experiment with changing the 6 in the random block to other numbers. The bigger the number, the flatter the settled snow.

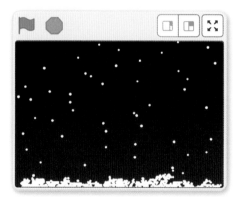

15 Now add a sprite for the snow to fall on. Click the sprite symbol 🐱 in the sprites list, and choose something from the library, such as the snowman. Add a new "if then" block to the code, as shown here, to make the snow stick to your sprite.

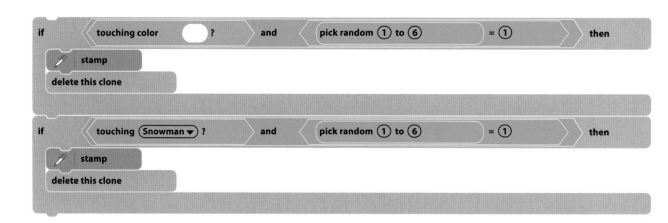

if ⟨ touching color ⬭ ? ⟩ and ⟨ pick random ① to ⑥ = ① ⟩ then
  🖊 stamp
  delete this clone

if ⟨ touching (Snowman ▼) ? ⟩ and ⟨ pick random ① to ⑥ = ① ⟩ then
  🖊 stamp
  delete this clone

Turbo Mode

If you're impatient to see the snow building up, you can speed things up by putting Scratch in "Turbo Mode." Hold down shift, and click on the green flag before you run the project. Scratch then runs the code much more quickly, with minimum time between blocks. Your snowdrift will now pile up much faster.

Shift-click the green flag to switch Turbo Mode on and off.

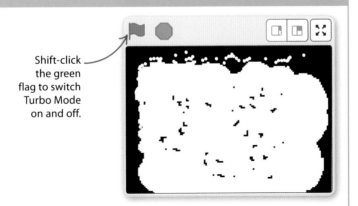

Secret pictures

It's easy to modify this project so that the snow sticks to an invisible object, slowly revealing it. Save your project as a copy before you try doing this.

16 Click on the paint symbol ✏ in the sprites list to create a new sprite. Name it "Invisible". Now use the paint editor to create your hidden object. It can be anything—a house, an animal, or someone's name—but make it big and use only one color. You can give the sprite more than one costume if you like.

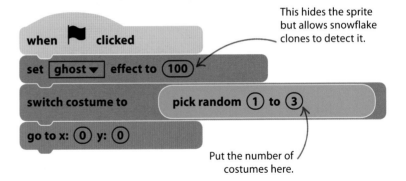

This hides the sprite but allows snowflake clones to detect it.

17 Add this code to the invisible sprite to position and hide it using the ghost effect. Using a "hide" block wouldn't work because that would stop snow from sticking to it.

```
when [flag] clicked
set [ghost ▼] effect to (100)
switch costume to (pick random (1) to (3))
go to x: (0) y: (0)
```

Put the number of costumes here.

18 Change the clone code to look like this. Now the snowflakes will settle only on the invisible sprite. They just disappear if they reach the bottom of the stage.

> Another snowy day! My favorite!

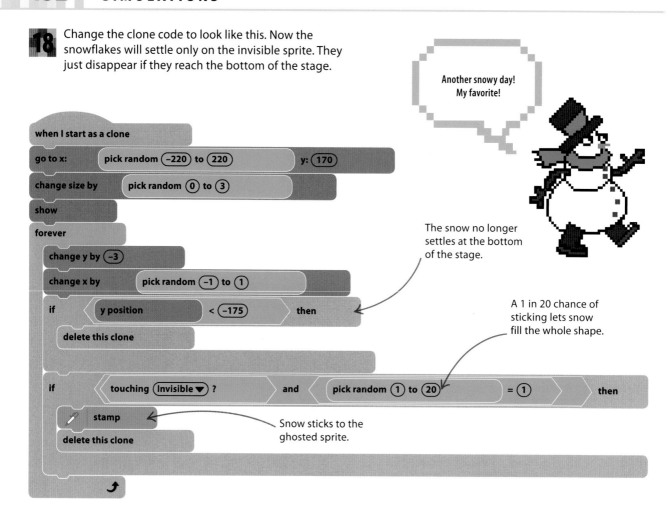

```
when I start as a clone
go to x:  pick random (-220) to (220)   y: (170)
change size by  pick random (0) to (3)
show
forever
    change y by (-3)
    change x by  pick random (-1) to (1)
    if   y position  <  (-175)  then
        delete this clone

    if   touching (Invisible ▼) ?  and  pick random (1) to (20)  = (1)  then
        stamp
        delete this clone
```

The snow no longer settles at the bottom of the stage.

A 1 in 20 chance of sticking lets snow fill the whole shape.

Snow sticks to the ghosted sprite.

19 Next, add a cool backdrop like "Winter" from the library, and watch your hidden shape appear in the snow. You can remove the "wait" block from the clone-making loop or use Turbo Mode to speed things up.

Hacks and tweaks

Falling snow or rain can make a great addition to any project or game. Try these hacks to send a snowstorm through your whole Scratch collection!

▷ **Sticky snowballs**
Occasionally, you might see clumps of snow just hanging in the sky. This starts when two snowflakes touch each other as they fall and stamp themselves in the sky. Once there, the clump grows as more snowflakes stick to it. If you follow the instructions in this project carefully, it shouldn't happen too often, but if it does, try experimenting with the numbers in the code. You can change the size and speed of the snowflakes, the amount they jiggle, and the delay between making each clone.

■ ■ **TRY THIS**

Starship

If you change the snowflake into a white or yellow dot and remove the random "change x" block that jiggles the falling snow, you get a starfield moving from the top to the bottom of the stage. Add a black backdrop, a spaceship, and some asteroids, and you've made a simple rocket game.

▽ **Adding snow to a project**
You can use the falling snow code blocks from steps 1–8 to add snow to another project—a great addition to a project like a Christmas card. The snow doesn't sense other sprites so is just a special effect. You'll need to add a "go to front layer" block to the start of the clone code to make the snowflakes fall in front of other sprites. Change the snowflake to a dark gray raindrop if you want to make it rain.

Add this block to the start of the existing code.

```
when I start as a clone

        go to  front ▼  layer

go to x:   pick random  (-220) to (220)      y: (170)
```

Fireworks Display

You might think you'd need lots of sprites to create a fireworks display, but Scratch's clones feature makes it easy. Clones are great for making explosions and other moving patterns. Computer graphics created with this technique are known as "particle effects."

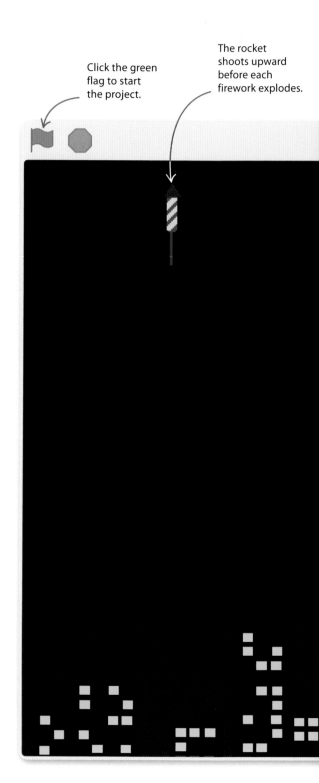

Click the green flag to start the project.

The rocket shoots upward before each firework explodes.

How it works

Click anywhere on the stage to make a rocket shoot up to that point and explode into a colorful firework. Each firework consists of hundreds of clones of a single sprite. The project uses simulated gravity to make the clones fall as they fly outward, while flickering or fading.

◁ **Rocket**

Each firework starts off as a rocket launched at the click of a mouse. You can use a simple colored line to represent the rocket or create a more detailed one in Scratch's paint editor.

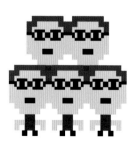

◁ **Clones**

To create the globes of colored "stars," this project uses 300 clones—the maximum number that Scratch allows. Each clone follows a slightly different path at a slightly different speed to make the stars spread out in a circle.

The stage flashes white at the moment of detonation.

Each explosion is made up of hundreds of clones that spread out from the rocket.

Find out how to add curving trails in the "Hacks and tweaks" section.

You can create your own backdrop for the fireworks display.

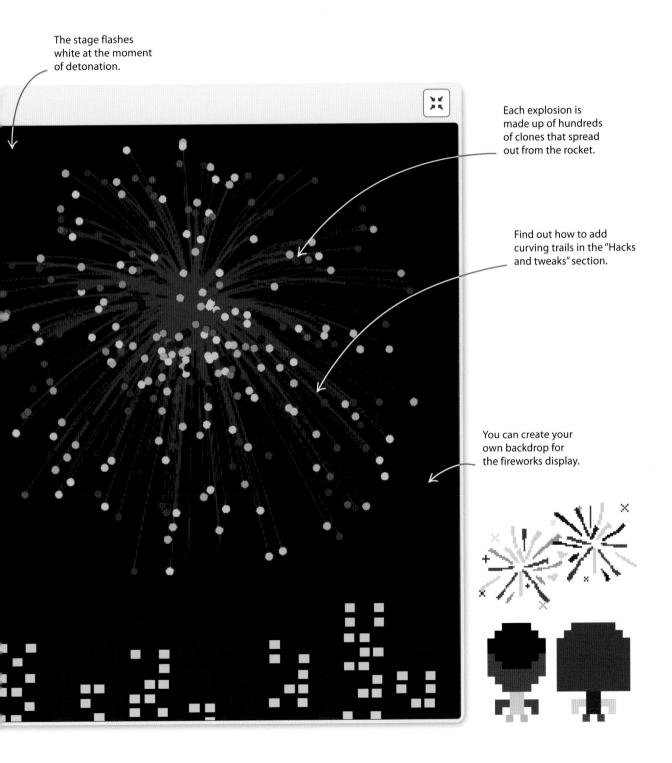

Creating the rocket

The first step in the project is to create the small rocket that shoots up into the sky and explodes in a blaze of fireworks. The code will make the rocket fly to wherever you click the mouse-pointer.

1 Start a new project, and delete the cat sprite by right-clicking on it and then selecting "delete". Click on the paint symbol ✎ in the sprites menu to create a new sprite and open the paint editor. Rename the sprite "Rocket".

2 Convert to Bitmap and use the line and brush tools to paint a rocket firework. A simple red line will do the job since the rocket will be small, but you can make it more realistic if you like.

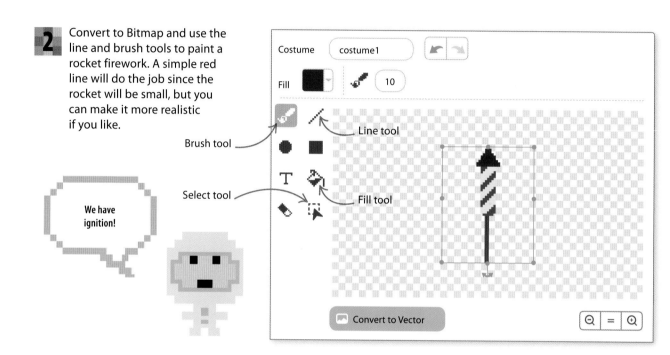

We have ignition!

Brush tool

Select tool

Line tool

Fill tool

3 When you're happy with the firework, use the select tool to drag a box around it. Then grab one of the corners and shrink the costume until it's no wider than 10 and no taller than 50. You can see the size in the costumes list.

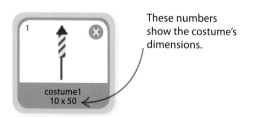

These numbers show the costume's dimensions.

4 Select the stage in the lower right of Scratch, and click on the Backdrops tab. Change the name of "backdrop1" to "Flash". This will provide a flash of light when a firework goes off. Click the paint symbol ✎ in the backdrops menu to create the main backdrop and call it "Night".

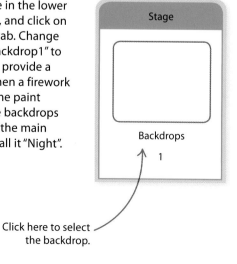

Click here to select the backdrop.

5 To make the night background more interesting, you can use two colors to create a gradient instead of filling it with solid black. Select the fill tool, and choose the two darkest blues in the vertical gradient. Then use the fill tool to paint the background so it's dark at the top but pale at the bottom. For extra decoration, add black and yellow rectangles to create a city skyline.

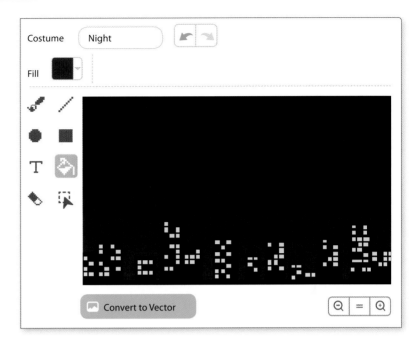

6 Next, select the rocket sprite, and add this code to make it shoot up to wherever the mouse is clicked.

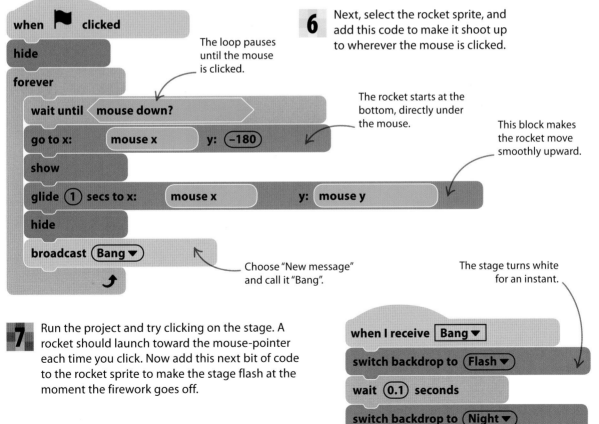

```
when [flag] clicked
hide
forever
    wait until < mouse down? >
    go to x: ( mouse x ) y: (-180)
    show
    glide (1) secs to x: ( mouse x ) y: ( mouse y )
    hide
    broadcast (Bang ▼)
```

The loop pauses until the mouse is clicked.

The rocket starts at the bottom, directly under the mouse.

This block makes the rocket move smoothly upward.

Choose "New message" and call it "Bang".

7 Run the project and try clicking on the stage. A rocket should launch toward the mouse-pointer each time you click. Now add this next bit of code to the rocket sprite to make the stage flash at the moment the firework goes off.

The stage turns white for an instant.

```
when I receive (Bang ▼)
switch backdrop to (Flash ▼)
wait (0.1) seconds
switch backdrop to (Night ▼)
```

Exploding stars

Real fireworks are packed with hundreds of "stars"—flammable pellets that glow with dazzling colors as they fly apart and burn. You can simulate the appearance of firework stars by using Scratch's clones feature. Follow the instructions here to create the stars and make them explode.

 8 Click the paint symbol ✎ in the sprites list to create a new sprite and call it "Stars". Before drawing it, select "Convert to Vector" in the bottom left of the paint editor, because using vector graphics will help keep the stars circular even when they are very small.

Make sure you select this.

9 Click the plus sign to zoom in since the costume will be very small. A simple green circle is all you need to create a star. Choose bright green in the color palette, and select the circle tool. To draw a circle, hold down the shift key on the keyboard as you drag.

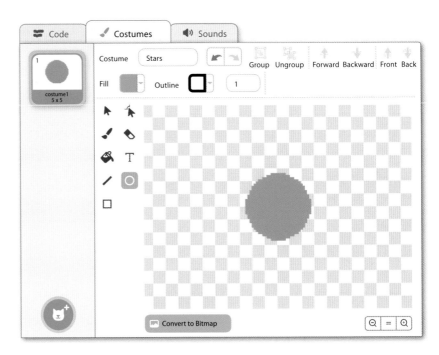

10 Look in the costumes list to check the circle's size—it needs to be about 5 x 5. If it's too large or small, choose the select tool ➤ and click on the green circle to make a box appear around it. Click on one of the corners and drag it to change the size.

costume1
5 x 5

11 Now add the following code to the stars sprite to create 300 hidden copies that will form the explosion.

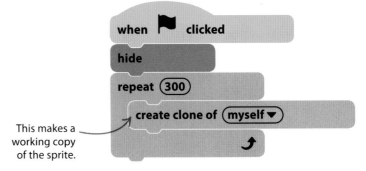

This makes a working copy of the sprite.

12 Click on Variables in the blocks palette and make a new variable called "speed". Choose "For this sprite only" in the dialogue box. This allows each clone to have its own copy of the variable with its own value, which makes each star unique. Uncheck the variable's check box so it doesn't appear on the stage.

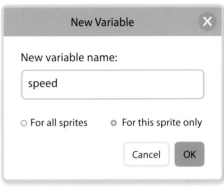

New Variable

New variable name:

speed

○ For all sprites   ● For this sprite only

Cancel   OK

13 Next, add this code to the stars sprite to create an explosion. Every clone will run its own copy of this code.

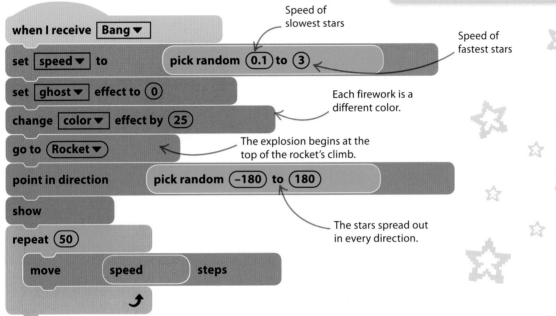

Speed of slowest stars

Speed of fastest stars

```
when I receive Bang ▼
set speed ▼ to (pick random (0.1) to (3))
set ghost ▼ effect to (0)
change color ▼ effect by (25)
go to (Rocket ▼)
point in direction (pick random (-180) to (180))
show
repeat (50)
    move (speed) steps
```

Each firework is a different color.

The explosion begins at the top of the rocket's climb.

The stars spread out in every direction.

14 Add this second "repeat" loop to the bottom of the code to make the stars slow down, fade away, and then disappear.

This block reduces the stars' speed a little with each repeat.

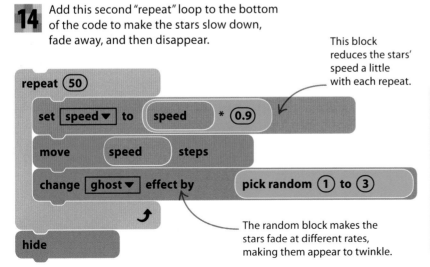

```
repeat (50)
    set speed ▼ to (speed * (0.9))
    move (speed) steps
    change ghost ▼ effect by (pick random (1) to (3))
hide
```

The random block makes the stars fade at different rates, making them appear to twinkle.

15 Try running the project. When the rocket explodes, you should see hundreds of colorful stars fly outward before fading.

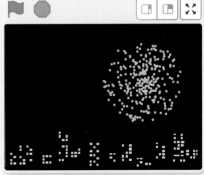

Hacks and tweaks

Try some of these changes to create new types of fireworks with multiple colors or trails. You can also use clones to create many other visual effects—or "particle effects," as computer artists call them.

▽ **Sticky stars**

You might sometimes see a trail of stars in a line if you send up a rocket right after running the project. This happens if the stars explode before all the clones are created. To fix the bug, add a "broadcast" block to the bottom of the "when flag clicked" code in the stars sprite and change the rocket's code to run only after it receives the message.

Stars sprite

```
when 🏴 clicked
hide
repeat 300
    create a clone of myself ▾
broadcast Ready ▾
```

Rocket sprite

```
when I receive Ready ▾
forever
    wait until       mouse down?
    go to x:    mouse x    y: -180
    show
    glide 1 secs to x:    mouse x    y:    mouse y
    hide
    broadcast Bang ▾
```

```
when 🏴 clicked
hide   ✕
```

▽ **Changing colors**

Fireworks makers use chemicals to create different colors. Try this hack to the stars sprite to make the colors change as the firework explodes.

The colors change as the firework expands.

```
when I receive Bang ▾
repeat 100
    change color ▾ effect by 2
```

Increase the number to see the colors change more quickly.

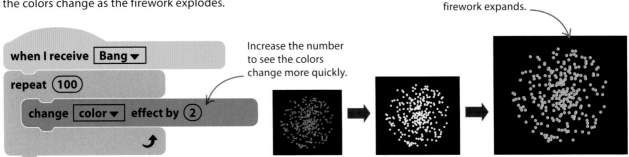

▽ Multicolored fireworks

Try the next hack to give each firework
stars with lots of different colors.

When the message is
received, every clone runs
its own copy of this code.

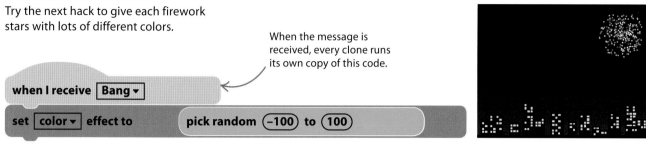

```
when I receive  Bang ▾

set  color ▾  effect to    pick random  (-100) to (100)
```

▷ Gravity trails

To make the stars arc downward
under the pull of gravity, leaving
colorful trails in their wake,
rebuild the code as shown here.
Remember to delete the original
code when you've finished. As
the timer increases, the stars
fall more quickly, which is how
gravity really works. See if you
can figure out how to change the
color of the trails or make them
brighten or fade out (hint: you'll
need to add the Pen extension).

The pen creates
the trails.

This sets the timer
to 0. It then counts
up in seconds.

The stars fall at an
ever greater speed as
the timer counts up.

This deletes
the trails.

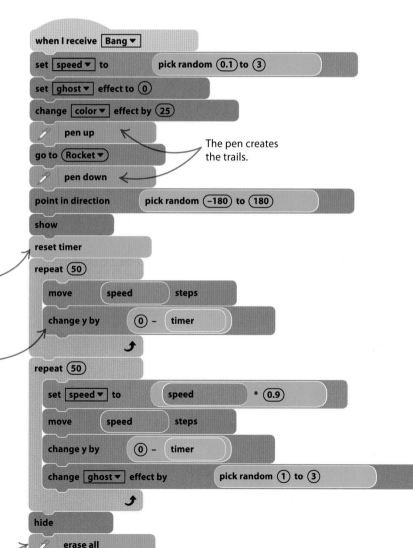

```
when I receive  Bang ▾

set  speed ▾  to           pick random (0.1) to (3)

set  ghost ▾  effect to (0)

change  color ▾  effect by (25)

    pen up

go to (Rocket ▾)

    pen down

point in direction       pick random (-180) to (180)

show

reset timer

repeat (50)

    move       speed       steps

    change y by       (0) -   timer
                          ↰

repeat (50)

    set  speed ▾  to           speed       * (0.9)

    move       speed       steps

    change y by       (0) -   timer

    change  ghost ▾  effect by       pick random (1) to (3)
                          ↰

hide

    erase all
```

Fractal Trees

You might think that drawing a tree requires an artistic eye and a lot of fussy work, but this project does the job automatically. The code creates special shapes called fractals, simulating the way that trees grow in nature.

Each leaf is a clone of the Scratch ball sprite.

How it works

When you run the project, a tree grows in a split second from the ground up. The tree is a fractal—a shape made from a repeating pattern. If you zoom in to just a part of a fractal, it looks similar to the whole shape. This repetition is easily generated in a computer program by using loops.

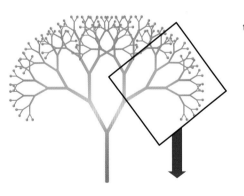

The branches get thinner and greener toward the ends.

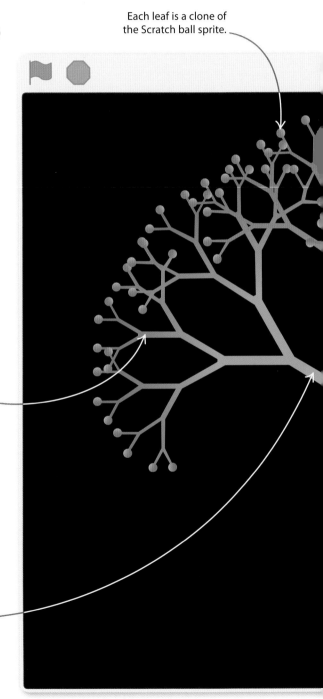

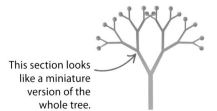

This section looks like a miniature version of the whole tree.

Branches are drawn with the Scratch pen.

A swarm of ball clones draws the tree, doubling in number after each layer of branches.

Click on this icon to escape the full-screen mode.

Romanesco broccoli

Lake Nasser in Egypt

Veins in the human body

△ **Fractals in nature**

Lots of natural objects have fractal shapes, including trees, river systems, clouds, blood vessels, and even broccoli. Natural fractals form most often when something keeps dividing into branches, which is how trees and blood vessels grow.

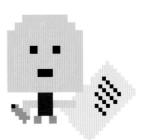

How it works

In the project Dino Dance Party, we saw how the ballerina's dance routine is based on an algorithm—a set of simple instructions that are followed in strict order. In this project, the code that draws the tree is also based on an algorithm. Try following the three steps below with a pen and paper.

1 Draw a straight line with a thick pen.

2 At the top of the line, draw two shorter, thinner lines at an angle—one to the left and one to the right.

3 Is the tree finished? If the answer is no, go back to step 2. Repeating these simple instructions in a loop creates a complicated pattern with hundreds of branches, just like a real tree.

Leaves and branches

Follow these steps to build a fractal tree, using Scratch's ball sprite for leaves and the Scratch pen to trace branches. The code creates new clones each time a branch divides, making more and more clones as the tree grows from a single trunk to a mass of twigs.

1 Start a new project and delete the cat sprite. Click on the sprite symbol 🐱 and add the ball sprite from the library. Rename it "Leaf". Open the Costumes tab, and choose the green costume.

Leaf

2 Click on Variables, and make the following variables for your project: "Angle", "Length", and "ShrinkFactor". Make sure to uncheck their boxes so they aren't shown on the stage.

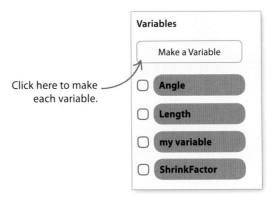

Click here to make each variable.

Variables

Make a Variable

⃝ **Angle**

⃝ **Length**

⃝ **my variable**

⃝ **ShrinkFactor**

3 Add this code to the leaf sprite. Remember, you'll need to add the Pen extension. You'll also need to create two new messages: "Draw Branch" and "Split Branch". Don't run it yet.

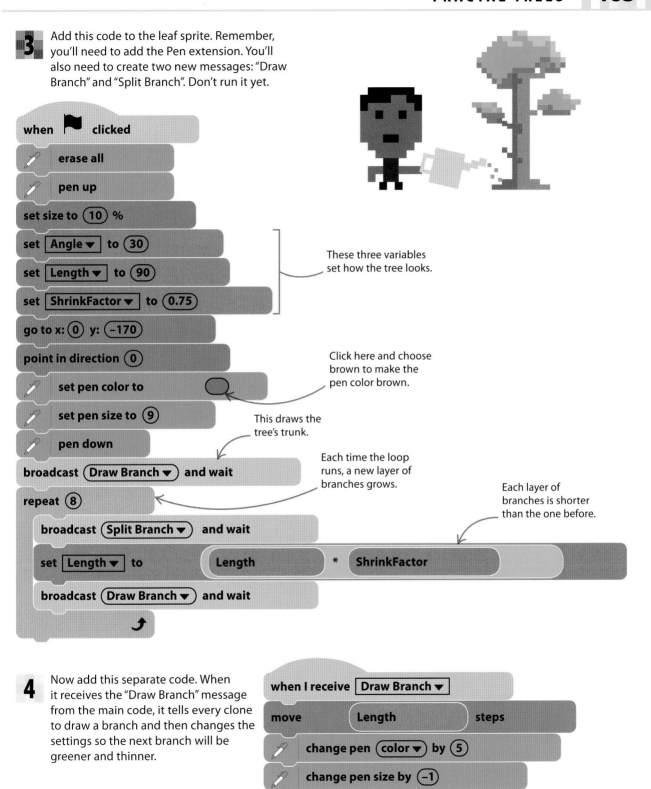

```
when [flag] clicked
    erase all
    pen up
    set size to (10) %
    set [Angle ▼] to (30)
    set [Length ▼] to (90)
    set [ShrinkFactor ▼] to (0.75)
    go to x: (0) y: (-170)
    point in direction (0)
    set pen color to ( )
    set pen size to (9)
    pen down
    broadcast (Draw Branch ▼) and wait
    repeat (8)
        broadcast (Split Branch ▼) and wait
        set [Length ▼] to (Length * ShrinkFactor)
        broadcast (Draw Branch ▼) and wait
```

These three variables set how the tree looks.

Click here and choose brown to make the pen color brown.

This draws the tree's trunk.

Each time the loop runs, a new layer of branches grows.

Each layer of branches is shorter than the one before.

4 Now add this separate code. When it receives the "Draw Branch" message from the main code, it tells every clone to draw a branch and then changes the settings so the next branch will be greener and thinner.

```
when I receive [Draw Branch ▼]
    move (Length) steps
    change pen (color ▼) by (5)
    change pen size by (-1)
```

5 Add the next bit of code to make the branches divide. It works by cloning each ball, forming a pair, and rotating them to face different directions. Once this code is run, there will be two clones at the end of every branch, each facing a different direction—ready to draw the next two branches.

The ball rotates to form an angle with the previous branch.

```
when I receive  Split Branch ▼
turn ↻  Angle              degrees
create clone of ( myself ▼ )
turn ↺  Angle              degrees
turn ↺  Angle              degrees
```

The ball rotates back twice as much, ready to draw the opposite branch.

6 Run the project, and you should create a beautiful tree. To make the "leaves" disappear and show only the twigs, click the red stop symbol on the stage.

Remember to use the full-screen mode.

"ShrinkFactor" controls how much shorter each branch is than the previous one (75 percent of the previous branch in this example).

"Angle" sets how far the branches spread apart at each split.

The "Length" variable sets the trunk's length in steps.

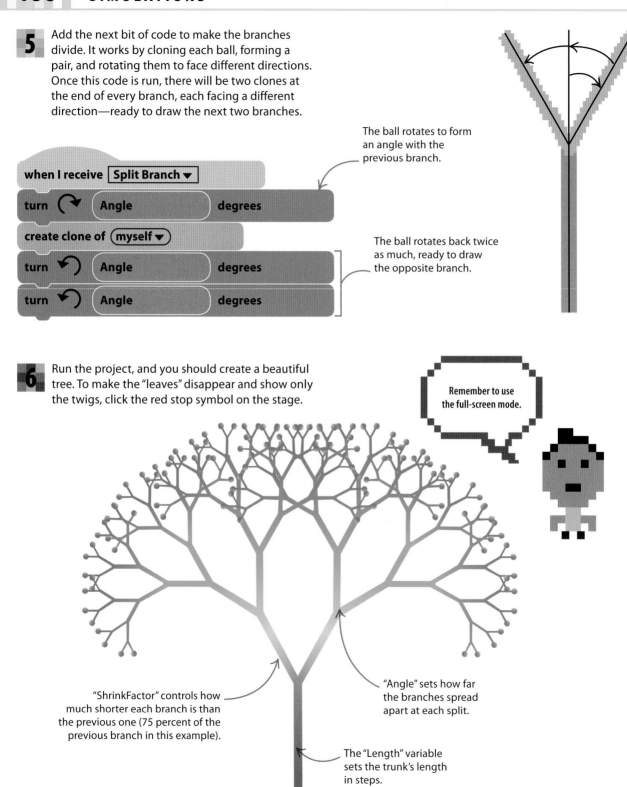

7 To make your tree stand out better, try changing the backdrop color.

Hacks and tweaks

You can change the settings used in this project to grow trees in amazingly varied shapes. You can also add a bit of randomness so that every tree is different.

▽ **Different angles**

Try experimenting with the value of "Angle" in the first orange block. You could also add a "pick random" block to generate randomly shaped trees. If you want to keep trees looking natural, set the minimum and maximum to 10 and 45. To make playing with the variable easier, check its box to show it on screen and turn it into a slider. You'll need to delete the "set Angle" block from the code if you do this.

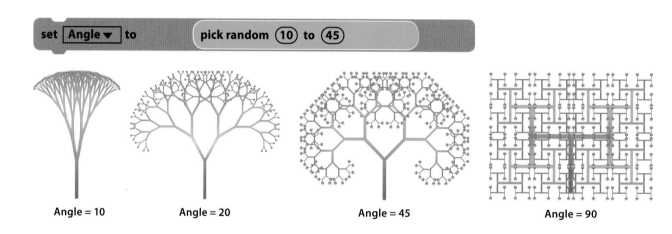

Angle = 10   Angle = 20   Angle = 45   Angle = 90

▽ **Ever-changing angles**

If you move the "set Angle" block inside the "repeat" loop, the angles between branches will change as the tree grows.

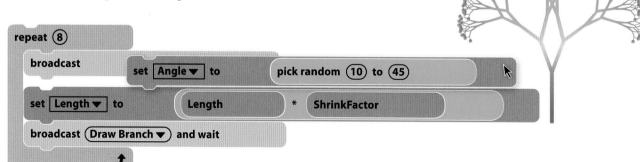

▽ **How tall is your tree?**

Try changing the values of "Length" and "ShrinkFactor", but be careful—it's easy to end up with very short trees or trees that are too big to fit on the stage.

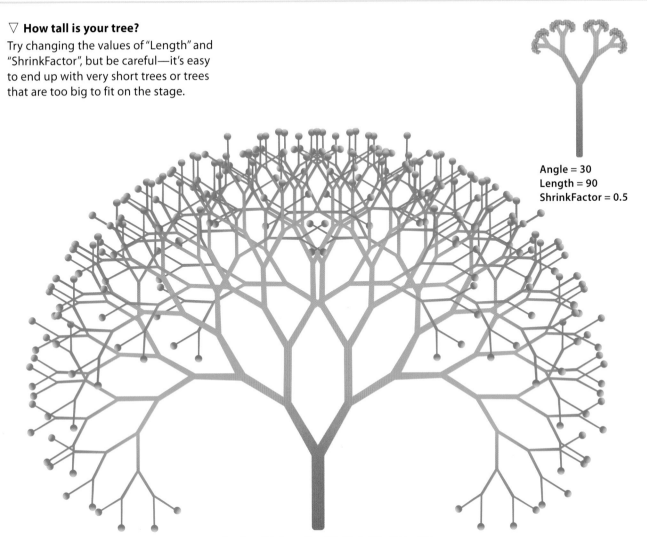

Angle = 30
Length = 90
ShrinkFactor = 0.5

Angle = 30, Length = 50, ShrinkFactor = 0.9

Change this number, or turn it into a variable set at the start of the code.

▽ **Don't run out of clones!**

The number inside the "repeat" loop controls how many times the branches split to create a new layer of branches. Eight is the maximum to get all the tiny twigs drawn because it uses 255 clones, and Scratch has a limit of 300 clones.

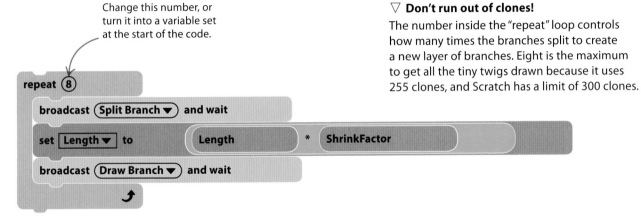

```
repeat (8)
    broadcast (Split Branch ▼) and wait
    set [Length ▼] to (Length * ShrinkFactor)
    broadcast (Draw Branch ▼) and wait
```

Grow a forest

You can adapt this project to grow trees wherever you click, covering the stage with a forest. Make the following changes to the code to do this.

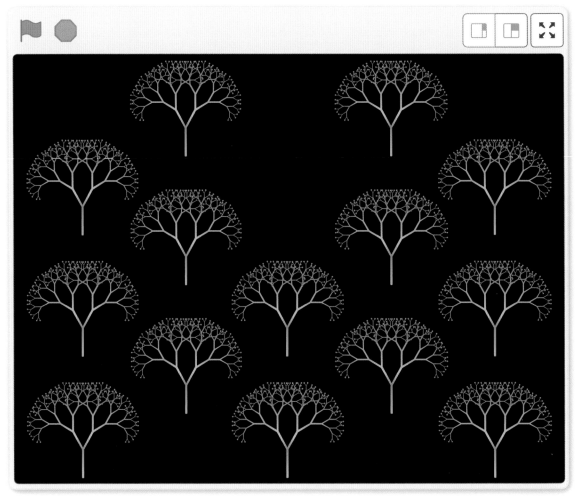

1 Add this code to stamp the leaves onto the tree before deleting the clones for the next tree.

Open the menu and create a new message called "Kill All Clones".

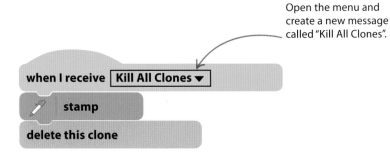

```
when I receive  Kill All Clones ▼
        stamp
delete this clone
```

2 Change the main code to look like this.

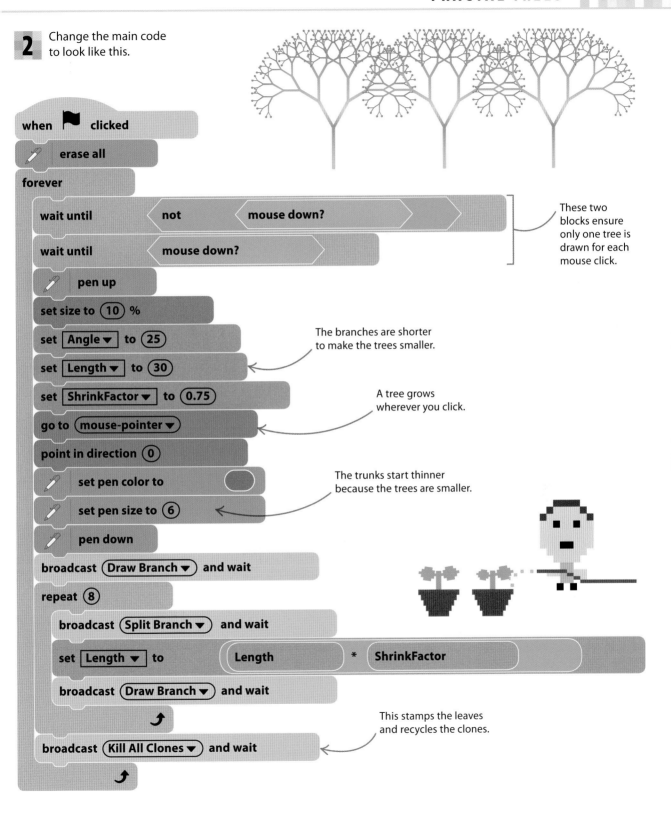

```
when 🏴 clicked
erase all
forever
    wait until    not    mouse down?
    wait until    mouse down?
    pen up
    set size to (10) %
    set Angle ▼ to (25)
    set Length ▼ to (30)
    set ShrinkFactor ▼ to (0.75)
    go to (mouse-pointer ▼)
    point in direction (0)
    set pen color to
    set pen size to (6)
    pen down
    broadcast (Draw Branch ▼) and wait
    repeat (8)
        broadcast (Split Branch ▼) and wait
        set Length ▼ to    Length * ShrinkFactor
        broadcast (Draw Branch ▼) and wait
    broadcast (Kill All Clones ▼) and wait
```

These two blocks ensure only one tree is drawn for each mouse click.

The branches are shorter to make the trees smaller.

A tree grows wherever you click.

The trunks start thinner because the trees are smaller.

This stamps the leaves and recycles the clones.

Snowflake Simulator

Snowflakes are famous for their amazingly varied shapes—it's said that no two are the same. Even so, all snowflakes share the same underlying structure, with six similar sides. This pattern, known as six-fold symmetry, makes snowflakes easy to mimic on a computer. You can use the same technique as in the Fractal Trees project, but this time every shape will be unique.

How it works

When you run this project, a snowflake appears on the stage. Later, you can make snowflakes appear wherever you click. Each snowflake is a bit like a fractal tree with six trunks. By using random numbers to set the lengths and angles of the white lines, you can create an endless variety of unique shapes—just like in nature.

△ **Real snowflakes**

Snowflakes are six-sided because they grow from ice crystals, which are hexagonal. As a snowflake grows, slight changes in air temperature affect the way ice crystals build up. Because every snowflake follows a different path and experiences different changes in temperature, every snowflake is unique.

△ **Snow-FAKE**

The drawing starts with six versions of the sprite to match the six-fold symmetry of a real snowflake. After that, the lines split in two repeatedly, like the fractal tree, but with more varied angles.

Symmetrical branches

To see how this project uses the ideas from Fractal Trees to make a snowflake, start by following these steps to create a simple, nonrandom snowflake.

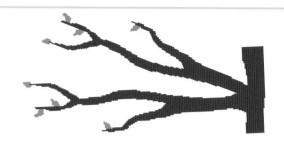

1 Start a new project and delete the cat sprite. Click on the paint symbol ✏ in the sprites list to create a new blank sprite. You don't need to paint a costume because all the drawing will be done by the code.

Sprite1

2 To make the snowflakes show up, paint the backdrop black. Select the stage in the lower right of Scratch and click the Backdrops tab above the blocks palette. Then click the fill tool in the paint editor and fill the paint area with black.

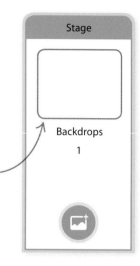

Click here to select the stage.

3 Click on Variables in the blocks palette and add five new variables to the project: "Angle", "Length", "Levels", "Symmetry", and "SymmetryAngle". Uncheck their boxes so that they don't show on the stage.

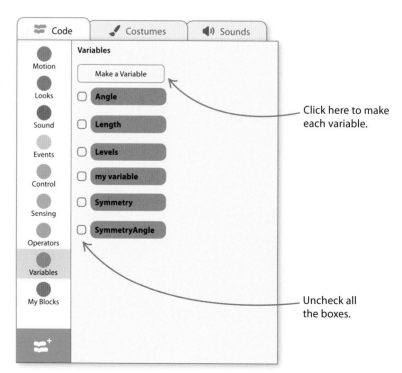

Click here to make each variable.

Uncheck all the boxes.

4 Select the sprite in the sprites list and give it the following code blocks. Remember to add the Pen extension. The code creates clones pointing in different directions to make a symmetrical pattern.

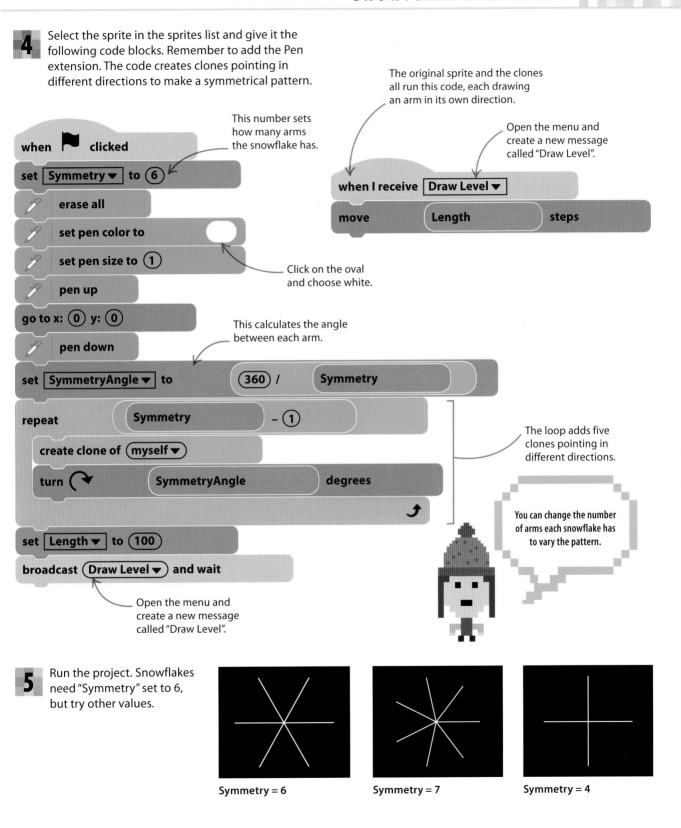

The original sprite and the clones all run this code, each drawing an arm in its own direction.

This number sets how many arms the snowflake has.

Open the menu and create a new message called "Draw Level".

```
when [flag] clicked
set Symmetry to 6
    erase all
    set pen color to (  )
    set pen size to 1
    pen up
go to x: 0 y: 0
    pen down
set SymmetryAngle to 360 / Symmetry
repeat Symmetry - 1
    create clone of myself
    turn ↻ SymmetryAngle degrees
set Length to 100
broadcast Draw Level and wait
```

```
when I receive Draw Level
move Length steps
```

Click on the oval and choose white.

This calculates the angle between each arm.

The loop adds five clones pointing in different directions.

You can change the number of arms each snowflake has to vary the pattern.

Open the menu and create a new message called "Draw Level".

5 Run the project. Snowflakes need "Symmetry" set to 6, but try other values.

Symmetry = 6

Symmetry = 7

Symmetry = 4

6 To fill in the rest of the snowflake, each clone will draw a succession of branching lines, like a fractal tree. Make the following changes to the main code, but don't run it yet.

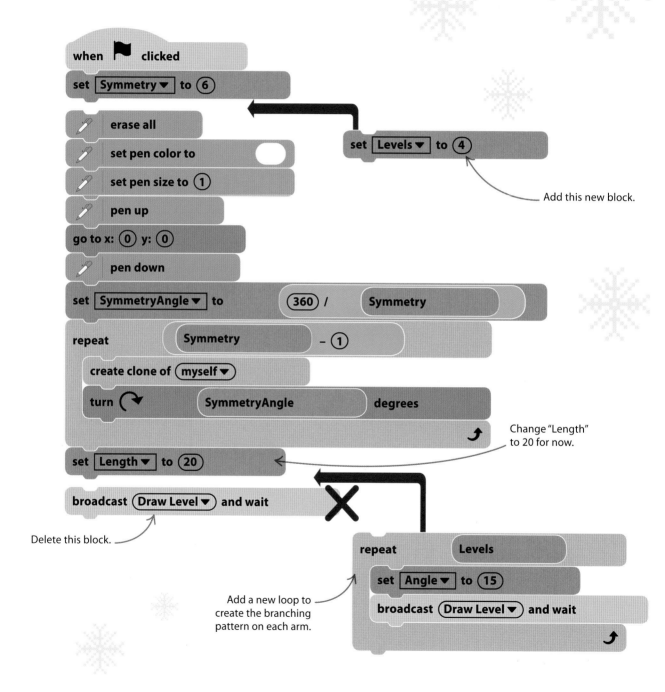

when ⚑ clicked

set [Symmetry ▼] to (6)

🖊 erase all

🖊 set pen color to ◯

🖊 set pen size to (1)

🖊 pen up

go to x: (0) y: (0)

🖊 pen down

set [SymmetryAngle ▼] to ((360) / (Symmetry))

repeat ((Symmetry) – (1))
  create clone of (myself ▼)
  turn ↻ ((SymmetryAngle) degrees)

set [Length ▼] to (20)

broadcast (Draw Level ▼) and wait

set [Levels ▼] to (4)

Add this new block.

Change "Length" to 20 for now.

Delete this block.

repeat (Levels)
  set [Angle ▼] to (15)
  broadcast (Draw Level ▼) and wait

Add a new loop to create the branching pattern on each arm.

7 Add three new blocks to the "When I receive" code to create new clones. These create a new clone and make the old and new clones face different directions.

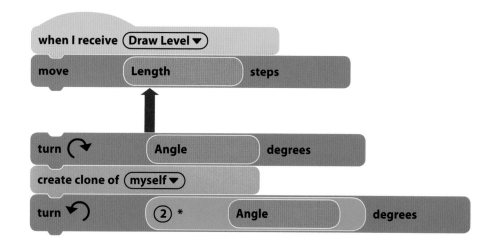

8 Now run the project. You'll see a branching snowflake like this.

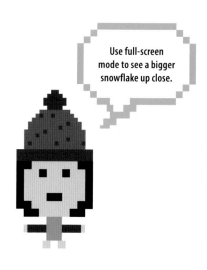

Use full-screen mode to see a bigger snowflake up close.

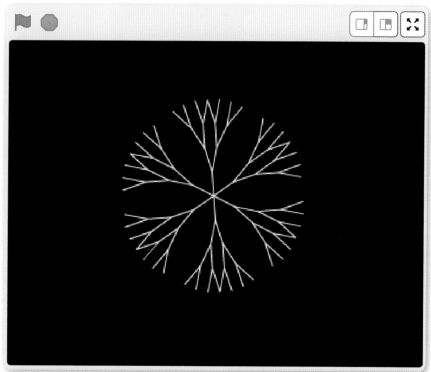

9 See what happens when you change the number of "Levels" in the "set" block at the top of the main code.

Levels = 1   Levels = 2   Levels = 3   Levels = 4

10 Now to make each snowflake different. Add some "pick random" blocks to the main code.

Add these new "pick random" blocks.

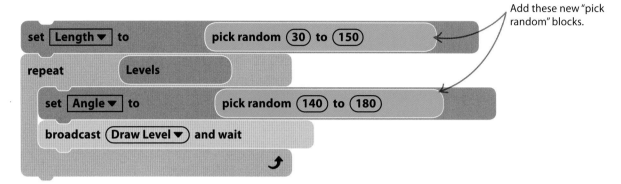

```
set Length ▼ to          pick random (30) to (150)
repeat          Levels
    set Angle ▼ to          pick random (140) to (180)
    broadcast (Draw Level ▼) and wait
```

 Run the project—you'll get a different snowflake every time.

Hacks and tweaks

Experiment! There are so many numbers to play with in this project; changing any one of them will give very different patterns. Play with the symmetry, levels, angles, and lengths. You can even add colors to your creations.

▷ **Odd flakes**
Try this quick change to make odd-looking snowflakes. It varies the line lengths after each branch point, creating a wider range of flaky weirdness.

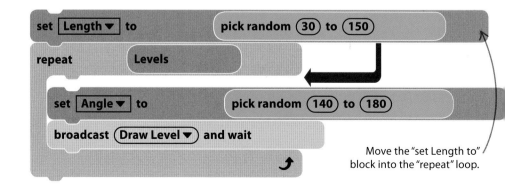

```
set Length ▼ to          pick random (30) to (150)
repeat          Levels
    set Angle ▼ to          pick random (140) to (180)
    broadcast (Draw Level ▼) and wait
```

Move the "set Length to" block into the "repeat" loop.

▽ Click-a-flake

Make snowflakes wherever you click on the stage with these modifications to the code. There's also code to clear the stage when you press the space bar in case things get too messy. Make sure you keep the code from step 7.

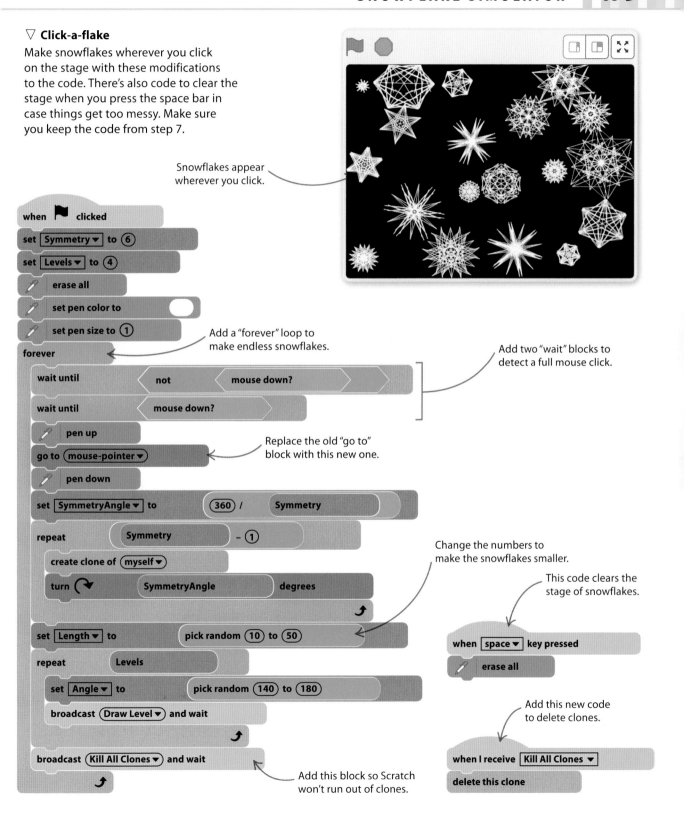

Snowflakes appear wherever you click.

when ⚑ clicked
set Symmetry ▾ to 6
set Levels ▾ to 4
🖊 erase all
🖊 set pen color to ⬭
🖊 set pen size to 1

Add a "forever" loop to make endless snowflakes.

forever
  wait until ⟨ not ⟨ mouse down? ⟩ ⟩
  wait until ⟨ mouse down? ⟩
  🖊 pen up
  go to mouse-pointer ▾
  🖊 pen down
  set SymmetryAngle ▾ to (360 / Symmetry)
  repeat (Symmetry - 1)
    create clone of myself ▾
    turn ↻ SymmetryAngle degrees
  set Length ▾ to pick random 10 to 50
  repeat Levels
    set Angle ▾ to pick random 140 to 180
    broadcast Draw Level ▾ and wait
  broadcast Kill All Clones ▾ and wait

Add two "wait" blocks to detect a full mouse click.

Replace the old "go to" block with this new one.

Change the numbers to make the snowflakes smaller.

Add this block so Scratch won't run out of clones.

This code clears the stage of snowflakes.

when space ▾ key pressed
🖊 erase all

Add this new code to delete clones.

when I receive Kill All Clones ▾
delete this clone

Music and sound

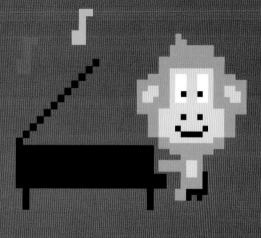

Sprites and Sounds

Do you have a younger brother or sister who's always trying to play on the computer? Here's something you can create in Scratch to keep the sibling amused. Click on any sprite for a unique action and sound. This project works especially well on a touchscreen computer.

How it works

Sprites and Sounds couldn't be easier to play—simply click the sprites or the background and you'll hear a sound and see an animation or visual effect.

▽ **Virtual circus**
This entertaining project is a mix of funny sounds and moves. You can add as many sprites and sounds as you want to spice up the show.

Each sprite performs its own little show when clicked.

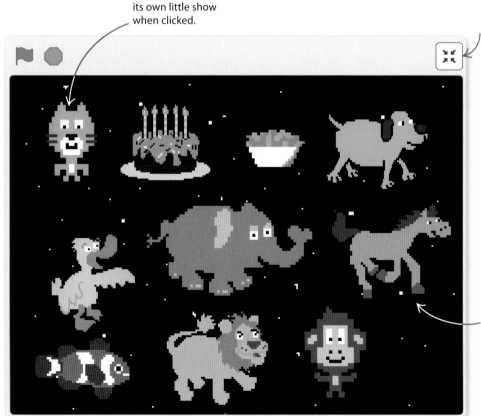

The project works best in full-screen mode, which prevents you from accidentally moving the sprites.

Click anywhere on the stage for some sound and action.

Background action

Everything in this project does something interesting when it's clicked, including the background. Follow these steps to create the background, and then start adding sprites.

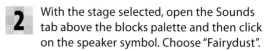

All together now!

1 Start a new project. Ignore the cat sprite for now and click on the backdrop symbol 🖼 in the lower right of the Scratch window to open the backdrop library. Load the "Stars" backdrop.

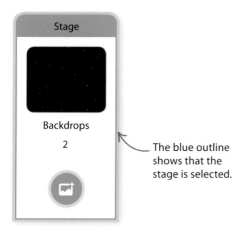

The blue outline shows that the stage is selected.

2 With the stage selected, open the Sounds tab above the blocks palette and then click on the speaker symbol. Choose "Fairydust".

This sound is 0.51 seconds long.

3 Now build this code for the stage to create some magic and sparkle when the backdrop is clicked. Make sure it works by clicking on the stage.

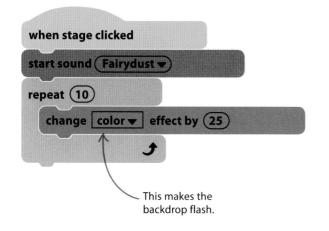

This makes the backdrop flash.

4 Drag the cat sprite to the top-left corner of the stage and add this code.

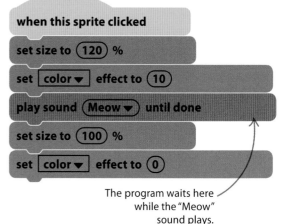

The program waits here while the "Meow" sound plays.

5 Click on the cat and see him grow, turn yellow, and meow before returning to normal.

The cat grows in size and changes its color.

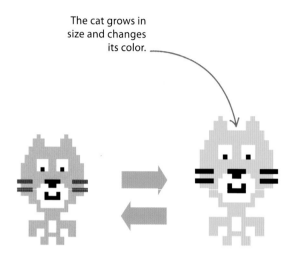

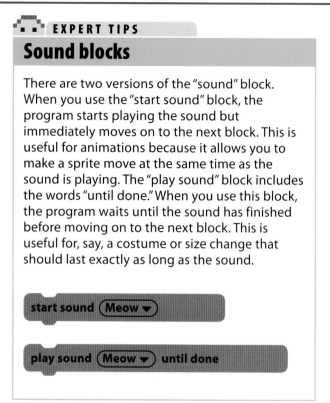

EXPERT TIPS

Sound blocks

There are two versions of the "sound" block. When you use the "start sound" block, the program starts playing the sound but immediately moves on to the next block. This is useful for animations because it allows you to make a sprite move at the same time as the sound is playing. The "play sound" block includes the words "until done." When you use this block, the program waits until the sound has finished before moving on to the next block. This is useful for, say, a costume or size change that should last exactly as long as the sound.

```
start sound Meow ▼
```

```
play sound Meow ▼ until done
```

Sprite extravaganza!

Now add the following sprites and their code blocks. Some of the sprites have the right sounds built in, but in other cases, you'll need to open the Sounds tab and load the sound from Scratch's sound library before you can select it in the code. After building each bit of code, position the sprite on the stage and test it.

6

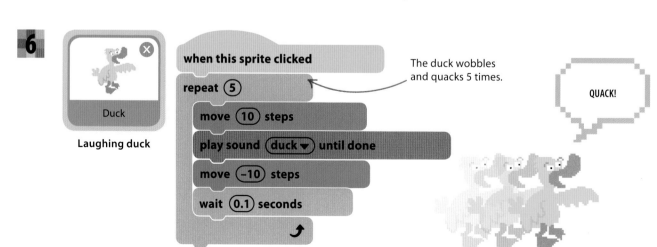

Duck

Laughing duck

```
when this sprite clicked
repeat 5
    move 10 steps
    play sound duck ▼ until done
    move -10 steps
    wait 0.1 seconds
```

The duck wobbles and quacks 5 times.

QUACK!

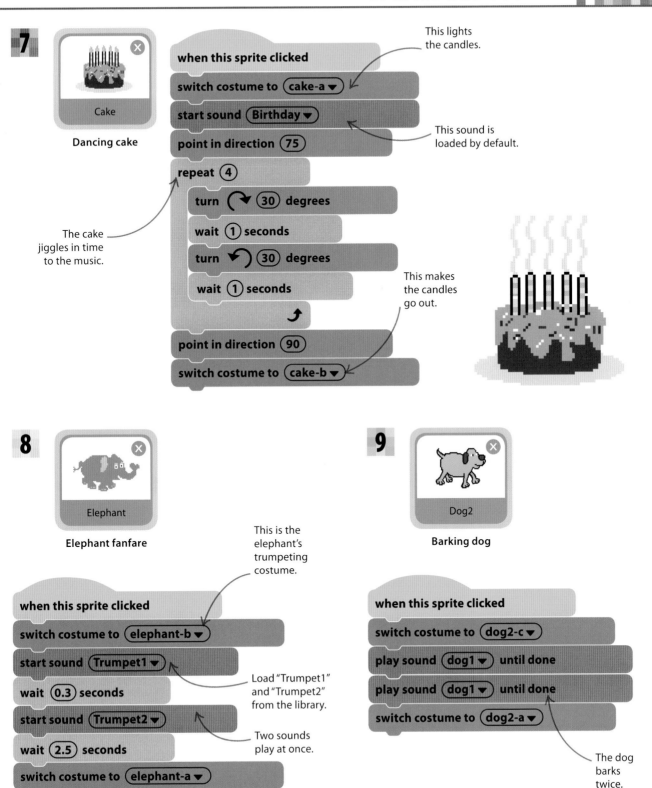

7

Cake

Dancing cake

when this sprite clicked
switch costume to (cake-a ▼)
start sound (Birthday ▼)
point in direction (75)
repeat (4)
  turn ↻ (30) degrees
  wait (1) seconds
  turn ↺ (30) degrees
  wait (1) seconds
point in direction (90)
switch costume to (cake-b ▼)

This lights the candles.

This sound is loaded by default.

The cake jiggles in time to the music.

This makes the candles go out.

8

Elephant

Elephant fanfare

This is the elephant's trumpeting costume.

when this sprite clicked
switch costume to (elephant-b ▼)
start sound (Trumpet1 ▼)
wait (0.3) seconds
start sound (Trumpet2 ▼)
wait (2.5) seconds
switch costume to (elephant-a ▼)

Load "Trumpet1" and "Trumpet2" from the library.

Two sounds play at once.

9

Dog2

Barking dog

when this sprite clicked
switch costume to (dog2-c ▼)
play sound (dog1 ▼) until done
play sound (dog1 ▼) until done
switch costume to (dog2-a ▼)

The dog barks twice.

10

Horse

Horsing about

when this sprite clicked

set rotation style | left-right ▾

switch costume to (horse-b ▾)

play sound (Horse ▾) until done

switch costume to (horse-a ▾)

start sound (Horse Gallop ▾)

repeat (16)

repeat (6)

move (5) steps

turn ↻ (180) degrees

The horse rears up and whinnies.

Load both sounds from the library.

The horse runs back and forth.

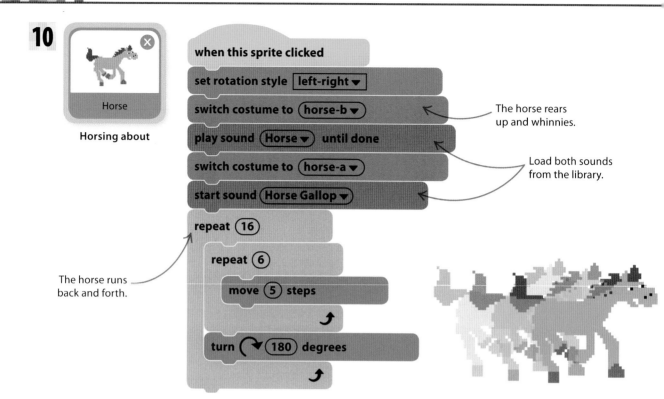

11

Fish

Chilling fish

when this sprite clicked

set rotation style | left-right ▾

start sound (bubbles ▾)

repeat (2)

point in direction (−90)

wait (1) seconds

point in direction (90)

wait (1) seconds

The "bubbles" sound is loaded by default.

The fish flips left and right calmly while the bubbles make a gurgling sound.

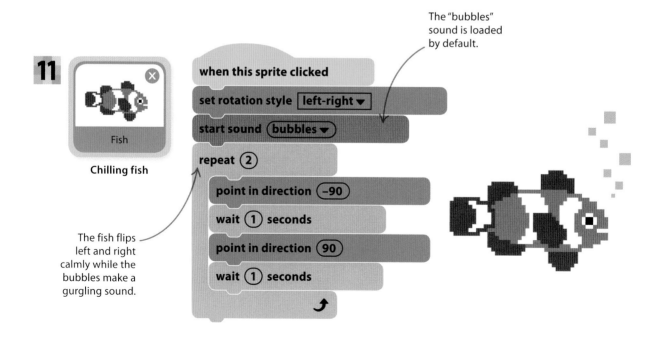

12

Lion

King of the jungle

13

Monkey

Jumpy monkey

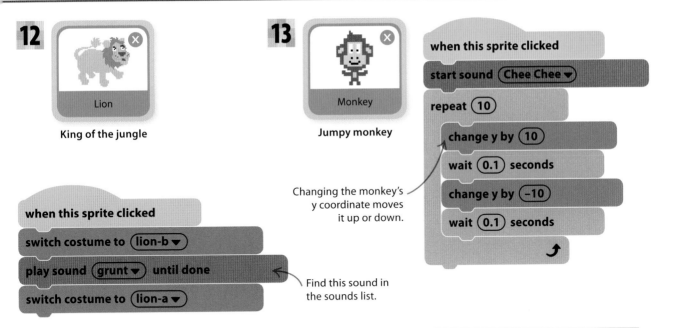

```
when this sprite clicked
start sound (Chee Chee ▼)
repeat (10)
    change y by (10)
    wait (0.1) seconds
    change y by (-10)
    wait (0.1) seconds
```

Changing the monkey's y coordinate moves it up or down.

```
when this sprite clicked
switch costume to (lion-b ▼)
play sound (grunt ▼) until done
switch costume to (lion-a ▼)
```

Find this sound in the sounds list.

Cheese puffs

The last sprite is a bowl of tasty-looking cheese puffs—when you click on the bowl, the cheese puffs will vanish. There isn't a suitable costume for the empty bowl, but you can create one using Scratch's paint editor. The following steps show you how.

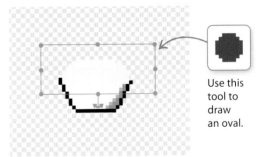

14 Add the "Cheesy Puffs" sprite from the library. Then click on the Costumes tab, and right-click (or control/shift-click) on the single costume shown and select "duplicate".

15 Select the duplicated costume "cheesy puffs2". In the paint editor, choose white or cream, and use the circle tool to draw an oval over the cheese puffs. Use the eraser tool to get rid of any leftover pieces.

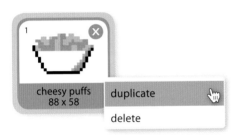

cheesy puffs
88 x 58

duplicate

delete

Use this tool to draw an oval.

16 Click the Sounds tab above the blocks palette, and load the "Chomp" sound from the library. Then give this code to the sprite.

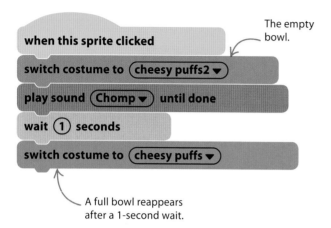

The empty bowl.

```
when this sprite clicked
switch costume to (cheesy puffs2 ▼)
play sound (Chomp ▼) until done
wait (1) seconds
switch costume to (cheesy puffs ▼)
```

A full bowl reappears after a 1-second wait.

17 Move all your sprites around so they fit nicely on the stage. Then test the project, but remember to click the full-screen symbol first so that the sprites don't accidentally move when you click them. Test every sprite. Note that you don't need to click the green flag to run this project, just click on the sprites.

Hacks and tweaks

This project is really a collection of mini-projects—one per sprite. This makes it easy to swap in new sprites or change animations and sounds. Have a look in Scratch's sprite and sound libraries for inspiration. You could also draw your own pictures or record your own sounds.

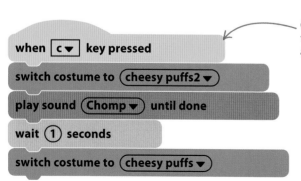

```
when [c ▼] key pressed
switch costume to (cheesy puffs2 ▼)
play sound (Chomp ▼) until done
wait (1) seconds
switch costume to (cheesy puffs ▼)
```

Change the header to trigger the code with a key instead of a click.

◁ **Animal piano**
For younger children, you could change the code blocks so that the animations and sounds are triggered by key presses instead of mouse clicks, turning the computer keyboard into a kind of piano. Choose keys that are widely spread to make the project into a game of "find the key."

▷ **Record your own sounds**

If your computer has a microphone, then you can give your project a personal touch by recording your own sounds. First, select the sprite you want to add a sound to—perhaps the lion, if you want to give him a better roar. Go to the Sounds tab, and click the microphone symbol 🎤 in the sounds menu. To start recording, click on the orange circle. To stop, click the square.

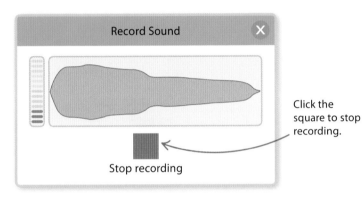

Click here to create a new sound.

Record

Click the circle to start recording.

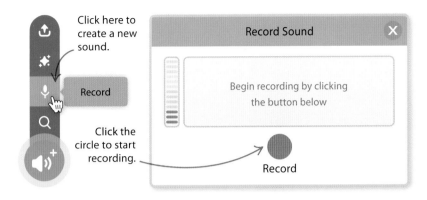

Record Sound

Begin recording by clicking the button below

Record

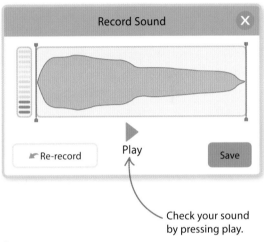

Record Sound

Click the square to stop recording.

Stop recording

Record Sound

Play

Re-record   Save

Check your sound by pressing play.

▷ **Editing sounds**

Scratch makes it easy to edit sounds that you've recorded or uploaded. Open the Sounds tab, and select the sound you want to work on. The pink pattern shows the volume of the sound as it plays. Use the "Trim" tool to highlight parts of the sound you want to delete or move, and then use the menus below to make changes or add effects.

Highlight parts of the sound you want to edit.

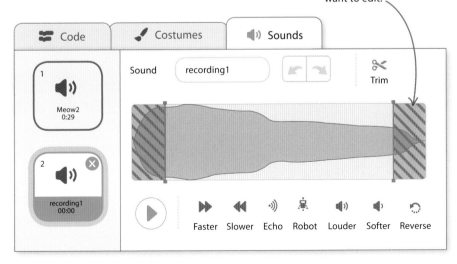

Code   Costumes   Sounds

1 — Meow2 0:29

2 — recording1 00:00

Sound   recording1   Trim

Faster Slower Echo Robot Louder Softer Reverse

Drumtastic

This project turns your computer keyboard into a drum machine. Type in anything you want, and Scratch turns the letters into repeating drum sounds using up to 18 different instruments, from cymbals and bongos to pounding bass drums.

How it works

When you run the project, the Scratch cat asks you to type something in the box. When you press return, the code turns each letter into a different sound and plays the phrase back over and over again. As the sounds play, the colored drums on the stage flash in time, while the Scratch cat walks to the beat.

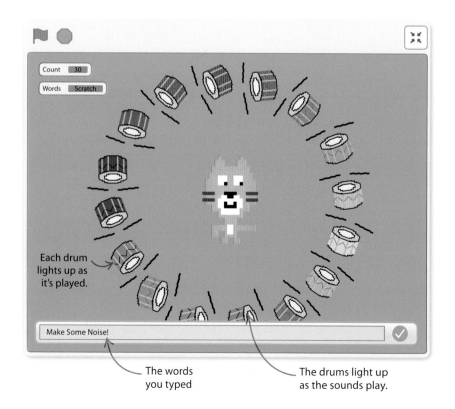

Each drum lights up as it's played.

The words you typed

The drums light up as the sounds play.

▽ **Scratch drumkit**
The code turns every letter into a drum sound. There are 26 letters in the alphabet, but Scratch has only 18 drum sounds, so some sounds are used for two letters.

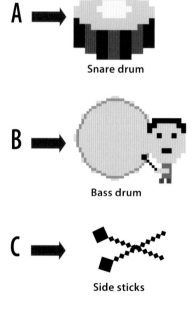

A ➡ Snare drum

B ➡ Bass drum

C ➡ Side sticks

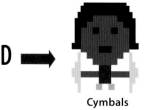

D ➡ Cymbals

Dancing cat

To make the project more fun, the cat will dance and shout out each letter in a speech bubble as the drums play. Follow the steps below to create a custom block that plays the drums and animates the cat.

1 Start a new project and keep the cat sprite. Set the background to a solid color by clicking the paint symbol ✔ in the backdrops menu, picking a cool color, and using the fill tool 🪣 to create a colored backdrop. Make sure you've clicked the "Convert to Bitmap" button.

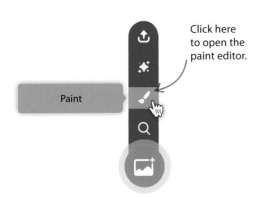

Paint

Click here to open the paint editor.

3 Now, create a custom block for the cat sprite. Choose "My Blocks" in the blocks palette and make a new block called "play a drum". This will trigger a code that plays a drum and makes the cat say the drum's letter at the same time. To keep things simple, the first version of the code will play the same drum sound every time.

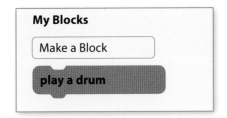

My Blocks

Make a Block

play a drum

4 The new block will appear in the blocks palette. Right-click (or control/shift-click) on this block, and choose "Edit" to add an input window for the drum's letter.

Type the name of the input here: "letter".

2 Select the cat sprite, click on Variables, and add these variables to your project: "Count" and "Words". Leave them checked so that they show on the stage.

Click here to make each variable.

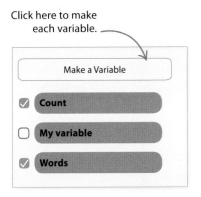

Make a Variable

☑ **Count**

☐ **My variable**

☑ **Words**

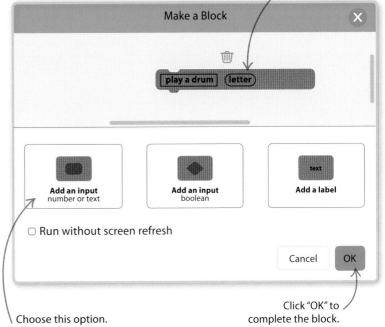

Make a Block

play a drum (letter)

Add an input
number or text

Add an input
boolean

Add a label
text

☐ Run without screen refresh

Cancel   OK

Choose this option.

Click "OK" to complete the block.

5 Next, add this code to the "define play a drum" header block. For now, the cat just says the letter, and the code plays only one type of drum: a snare drum. The code will get longer later so that different drums can play. Add the Music extension by clicking "Add Extension" at the bottom left and choosing "Music" to use the play drum blocks.

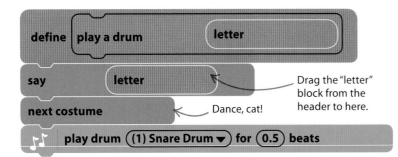

Drag the "letter" block from the header to here.

Dance, cat!

LINGO

Strings

Programmers call a sequence of words or letters a string. Think of the letters as being strung together like beads on a necklace.

6 Now add the code below to ask the user to type something on the keyboard. This code sends the letters one at a time to the cat using the "play a drum" block. Anything set as an input in the "play a drum" block is put in the blue "letter" block in the define code.

A, B, C, D, E ...

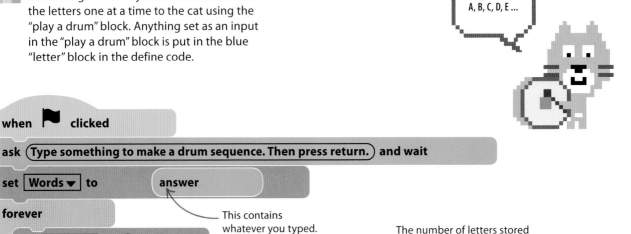

This contains whatever you typed.

The number of letters stored in the variable "Words".

With each loop, a different letter is set as the input in the "play a drum" block.

On to the next letter.

7 Run the project. Type "Scratch" and press enter. The cat will shout out the letters of "Scratch" to a drumbeat.

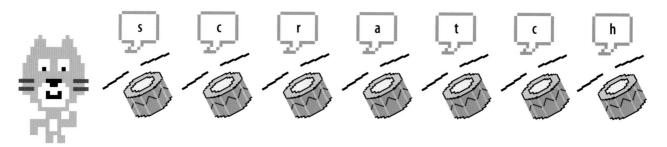

From letters to drums

The next step is to change the code so that each letter plays a particular drum. Scratch has only 18 drum sounds, so some sounds will be played by more than one letter. Spaces and punctuation will create brief pauses in the pattern of drums. Scratch also ignores whether letters are capitals or not—"A" and "a" are treated the same.

play drum ((1) Snare Drum ▼) **for** (0.25) **beats**

Scratch's "play drum" block has 18 built-in sounds.

✓ (1) Snare Drum	**a, s**
(2) Bass Drum	**b, t**
(3) Side Stick	**c, u**
(4) Crash Cymbal	**d, v**
(5) Open Hi-Hat	**e, w**
(6) Closed Hi-Hat	**f, x**
(7) Tambourine	**g, y**
(8) Hand Clap	**h, z**
(9) Claves	**i**
(10) Wood Block	**j**
(11) Cowbell	**k**
(12) Triangle	**l**
(13) Bongo	**m**
(14) Conga	**n**
(15) Cabasa	**o**
(16) Guiro	**p**
(17) Vibraslap	**q**
(18) Cuica	**r**

8 First, you need to add four new variables: "Alphabet", which stores the whole alphabet in order; "AlphabetCount", which stores a letter's numerical position in the alphabet from 1 to 26; "NumberOfDrums", for the number of different drum sounds in Scratch; and "ChosenDrum", to hold the number of the drum sound to be played.

Uncheck the boxes so that the variables don't appear on stage.

Alphabet

AlphabetCount

ChosenDrum

NumberOfDrums

9 Add three new blocks to the start of the main code to set up the "Alphabet" and "NumberOfDrums" variables. The "Draw Drums" message will trigger code that draws the drums, but that code comes later.

Scratch has 18 different drum sounds.

Type the alphabet in order here.

Open the menu to create a new message and call it "Draw Drums".

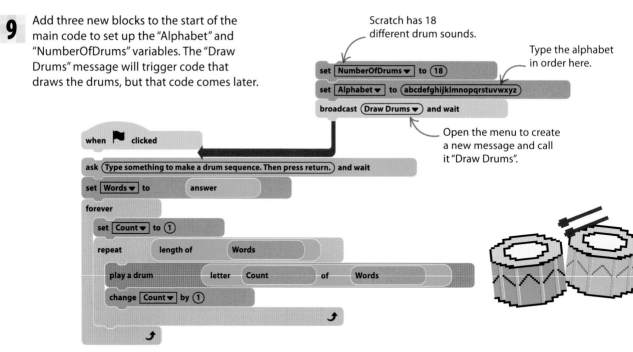

10 Add this code to the definition of "play a drum". It converts each letter into a number and then uses that to play the correct drum sound. If no match is found, then a short pause, or "rest," is used instead.

Delete the block.

Start at "A".

This loop scans the alphabet for a match in order to convert the letter into a number.

Play the chosen drum sound.

Is the chosen number bigger than the number of drums? Move it back into range.

On to the next letter of the alphabet.

No drum picked? Just take a short break.

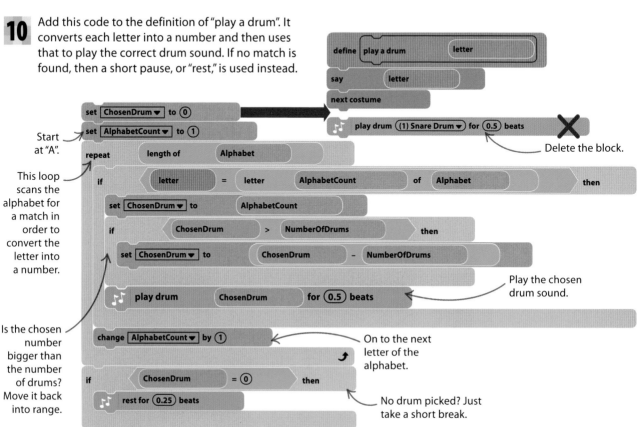

11 Now run the project and see if you can create some cool drumbeats. Try "a a a a abababab," for instance. Remember you can use spaces or punctuation marks to create pauses.

Light-up drums

To make the project look more interesting, you can add a circle of 18 colored drum clones— one for each sound. Each drum will light up when its sound plays.

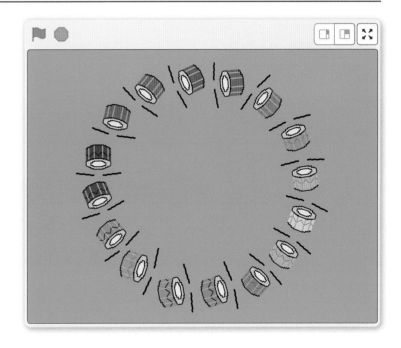

12 Click on the sprite symbol 🐱 in the sprites list and add the Drum sprite from the library.

13 Add a variable called "drumID", making sure you select "for this sprite only"—this lets every clone have its own copy of the variable. This variable will hold a unique ID number for each drum to help it light up at the right time. Uncheck this variable so it doesn't show on the stage.

New Variable

New variable name:

drumID

○ For all sprites   ● For this sprite only

Cancel   OK

Choose this option, or the drums won't work properly.

14 Add the code below to the Drum sprite. When this code receives the "Draw Drums" message, it draws a ring of colored drum clones on the stage, each with a unique ID number.

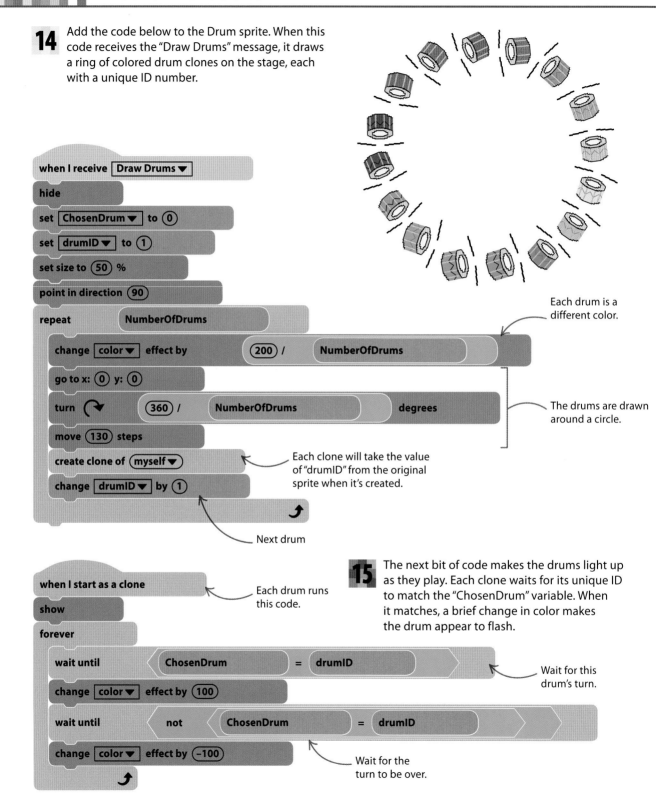

```
when I receive  Draw Drums ▼

hide

set  ChosenDrum ▼  to  0

set  drumID ▼  to  1

set size to  50  %

point in direction  90

repeat            NumberOfDrums

    change  color ▼  effect by        200  /      NumberOfDrums

    go to x:  0  y:  0

    turn ↻            360  /      NumberOfDrums          degrees

    move  130  steps

    create clone of  myself ▼

    change  drumID ▼  by  1
```

Each drum is a different color.

The drums are drawn around a circle.

Each clone will take the value of "drumID" from the original sprite when it's created.

Next drum

15 The next bit of code makes the drums light up as they play. Each clone waits for its unique ID to match the "ChosenDrum" variable. When it matches, a brief change in color makes the drum appear to flash.

```
when I start as a clone

show

forever

    wait until      ChosenDrum        =      drumID

    change  color ▼  effect by  100

    wait until      not      ChosenDrum        =      drumID

    change  color ▼  effect by  -100
```

Each drum runs this code.

Wait for this drum's turn.

Wait for the turn to be over.

16 Run the project. The drums should light up in time to the sequence. Try the sequence "abcdefghijklmnopqrstuvwxyz" to see all the drums work in order and to see how the drums are reused after "r."

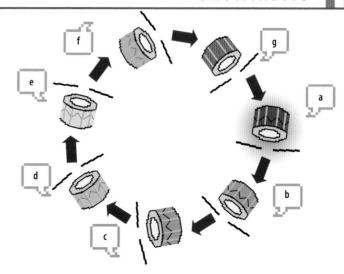

Hacks and tweaks

Being able to create a sequence that controls something is very useful. You could adapt this idea to make an automatic piano, singing ducks, or an on-screen robot that follows a program in the form of letter sequences.

▽ **Tempo**
The pace at which music plays is called its tempo. The higher the tempo, the shorter the beat and the faster the music. Scratch has a handy tempo setting—you'll find it in the Music section of the blocks palette. Check the tempo box to display it on stage. Add these code blocks to the drum sprite so that you can change the tempo with the arrow keys. The space bar will reset the tempo to 60 beats per minute.

· · TRY THIS

Word piano

If you change the "play drum" block to a "play note" block, you can create a singing animal. You'll need to set the total number of available notes to 26 so that every letter has its own note.

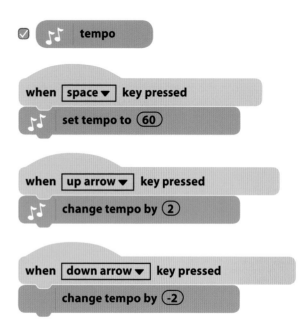

Mindbenders

The Magic Spot

Run this project and stare at the cross in the middle while the pink spots around it flash on and off. Within a few seconds, a ghostly green spot will appear among the pink ones, but it isn't actually there. Scratch gets mysterious with this amazing optical illusion.

How it works

The spots take turns to disappear and reappear very quickly, causing a gap in the circle that races around. This confuses your brain, which fills in the missing spot with a different color, creating a magic green spot that doesn't exist. Keep watching, and the magic green spot will erase all the pink spots, but this is just an illusion, too!

△ **Clones with identity**
Each circle is a clone. In this project, you'll see how each clone can have its own copy of a variable—in this case, an ID number that's used to control which circle is hidden at any moment.

Keep your eyes fixed on the cross to see the illusion.

This illusion works best in full-screen mode.

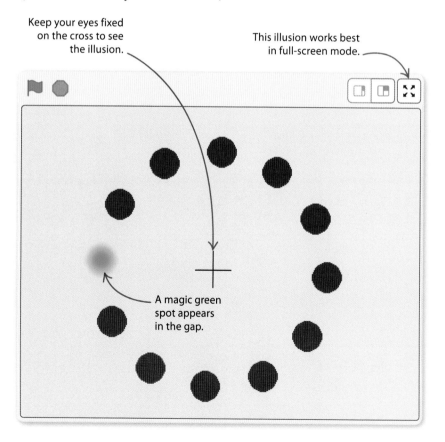

A magic green spot appears in the gap.

△ **Color in your brain**
This kind of illusion is called an afterimage. If you stare at something for a long time without moving your eyes, the color receptors in your eyes tire and your brain starts to tune colors out. So when the color suddenly disappears, you briefly see a negative afterimage—a sort of "color hole."

Pink costume

A single sprite is all that's needed to make this illusion, but first you'll need to draw the pink spot and black cross as costumes.

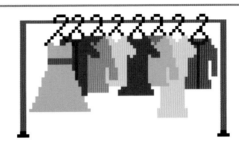

1 Start a new project and remove the cat sprite. Click on the paint symbol ✏ in the sprites menu to draw a new sprite. Select the bright pink color in the color palette.

Make sure you choose this color or the illusion might not work properly.

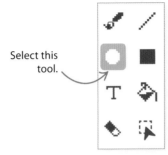

Fill

Color 85

Saturation 70

Brightness 100

2 Select the circle tool, and make sure the "Filled" option is selected at the top of the painting area. Make sure you are in Bitmap mode.

Select this tool.

Filled   Outlined

3 Click near the middle of the paint editor, and drag the mouse while holding the shift key on the keyboard to paint a solid pink circle. Make sure you position the circle on the small cross in the middle of the painting area.

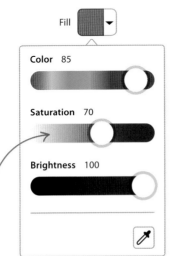

Hold down the shift key to avoid making an oval.

4 Your newly drawn spot will appear in the costumes list. The numbers under its name tell you its size. You need a spot about 35 x 35 in size, but don't worry if it's wrong—the next step shows you how to resize it.

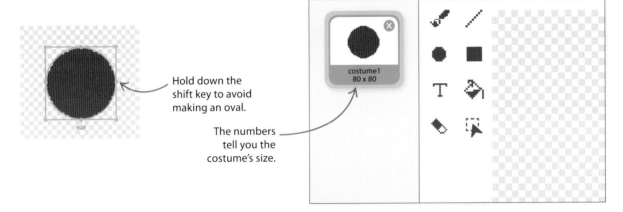

costume1
80 x 80

The numbers tell you the costume's size.

5 If it's too big or too small, drag one of the corners of the box that appears around it to resize the circle. If the box disappears, use the select tool to draw it around the circle again. Name this costume "Spot" at the top of the paint editor.

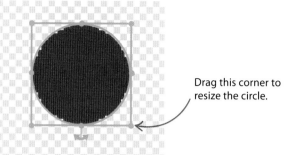

Drag this corner to resize the circle.

Name the costume "Cross".

6 The next step is to create the black cross that appears in the middle of the illusion. Click the paint symbol ✏ in the costumes menu to start drawing a new costume and then use the line tool to make a black cross about half as big as the spot. To draw perfectly horizontal and straight lines, hold down the shift key.

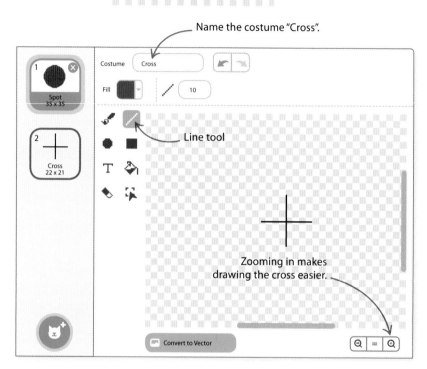

Line tool

Zooming in makes drawing the cross easier.

Circle of clones

Now to fill in the background and create the circle of clones. The code will give each clone a unique identification number that will make it easy to hide.

7 To create the correct backdrop for the illusion, click on the paint symbol ✏ in the backdrops menu in the lower right of Scratch.

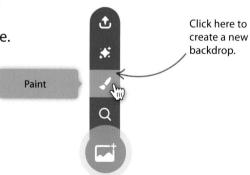

Click here to create a new backdrop.

Paint

8 Now select this gray color. Make sure you get the exact shade, or the illusion might not work properly. Use the fill tool 🪣 to create a gray backdrop. Just click anywhere in the paint area.

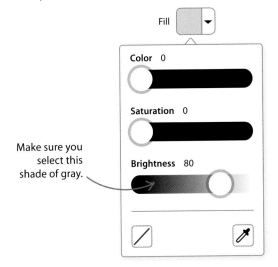

Fill

Color 0

Saturation 0

Make sure you select this shade of gray.

Brightness 80

9 Click on the sprite and select the Code tab. Choose Variables in the blocks palette and click on "Make a Variable". Create a variable called "id" and select the option "For this sprite only". This is important because it allows each clone to have its own copy of the variable with its own value. Uncheck the box in the blocks palette so that the variable doesn't show on the stage.

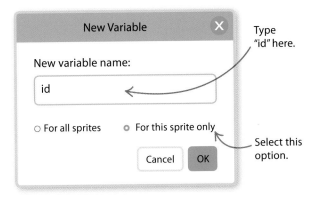

New Variable ✕

Type "id" here.

New variable name:

id

○ For all sprites ● For this sprite only

Select this option.

Cancel   OK

10 Now add the two code blocks shown here to create 12 clones of the pink spot arranged in a circle. When a clone is created, it gets a copy of the original sprite's "id" variable, which means each clone has a unique number.

The "repeat" loop runs once for each spot.

A cloned spot is made.

This temporary code shows that each clone has its own "id" number.

The sprite moves back to the center.

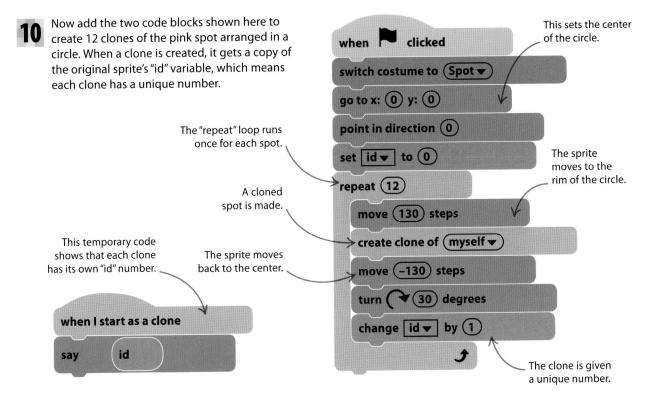

This sets the center of the circle.

when 🏳 clicked

switch costume to (Spot ▾)

go to x: (0) y: (0)

point in direction (0)

set [id ▾] to (0)

repeat (12)

move (130) steps

create clone of (myself ▾)

move (−130) steps

turn ↻ (30) degrees

change [id ▾] by (1)

The sprite moves to the rim of the circle.

The clone is given a unique number.

when I start as a clone

say   id

11 Run the project, and each clone will say its own value of "id." Each will be different, counting 0–11 around the circle.

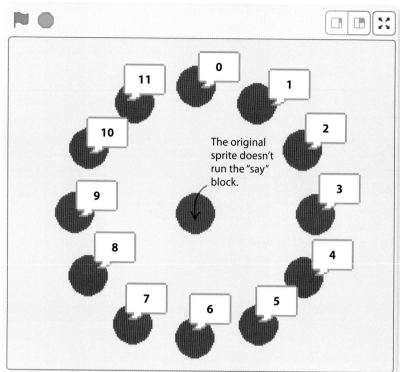

The original sprite doesn't run the "say" block.

12 Now delete the smaller code because you don't need to see those speech bubbles during the illusion.

Delete this code.

Creating the illusion

Now, to make the code hide each of the spots in turn, you'll need to make a new variable, called "Hidden", that will specify which clone should hide.

13 Click the orange Variables block in the blocks palette and make a new variable. Call it "Hidden". Uncheck its box in the blocks palette so that the variable doesn't appear on the stage.

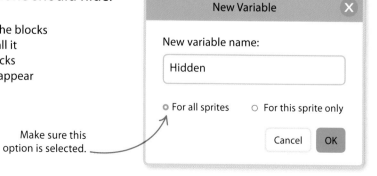

New Variable

New variable name:

Hidden

● For all sprites   ○ For this sprite only

Make sure this option is selected.

Cancel   OK

14 Add the blocks shown below to the bottom of the sprite's code, but don't run the project yet.

15 Now add this separate code to the sprite. All the clones run this code. Only the clone whose "id" number matches the "Hidden" variable will hide. As the value of "Hidden" rises, each spot hides in turn.

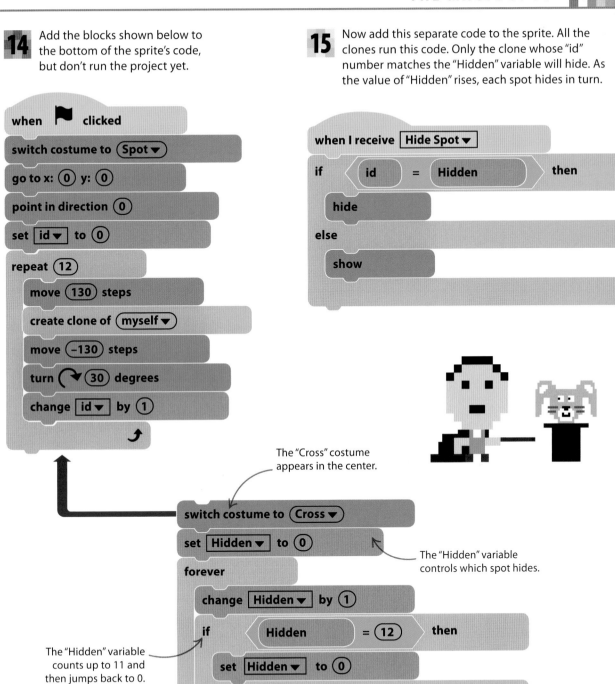

```
when [flag] clicked
switch costume to (Spot ▼)
go to x: (0) y: (0)
point in direction (0)
set [id ▼] to (0)
repeat (12)
    move (130) steps
    create clone of (myself ▼)
    move (-130) steps
    turn ↻ (30) degrees
    change [id ▼] by (1)
```

```
when I receive (Hide Spot ▼)
if < (id) = (Hidden) > then
    hide
else
    show
```

The "Cross" costume appears in the center.

```
switch costume to (Cross ▼)
set [Hidden ▼] to (0)
forever
    change [Hidden ▼] by (1)
    if < (Hidden) = (12) > then
        set [Hidden ▼] to (0)
    broadcast (Hide Spot ▼)
    wait (0.1) seconds
```

The "Hidden" variable controls which spot hides.

The "Hidden" variable counts up to 11 and then jumps back to 0.

This number controls the speed at which the magic spot moves around the circle.

Open the menu and create a new message called "Hide Spot".

16 Run the project. You should see the gap move around the circle. Put the stage into full-screen mode and stare at the cross. Within a few seconds, you'll see the magic green spot. Keep staring at the cross, and the magic spot will start to erase the pink spots. When you look away from the cross, you'll just see the empty gap again.

Stare at the cross to see the illusion.

The magic spot vanishes if you look directly at it.

I'm seeing things!

EXPERT TIPS

If then else

The "if then" block is very useful for either running or skipping a group of blocks depending on the answer to a question. But what if you want to do one thing for yes (true) and another for no (false)? You could use two "if then" blocks, but programmers face this problem so often that they created another solution: "if then else." The "if then else" block has two jaws, for two sets of blocks. The top set runs on yes; the bottom set runs on no.

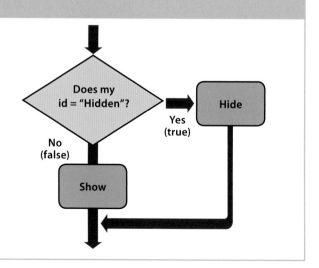

Does my id = "Hidden"?

Yes (true) → Hide

No (false)

Show

Hacks and tweaks

You can use Scratch to investigate this curious optical illusion further. Would the illusion still work if you change the color of the spots or background or change the speed? What if there were more spots or more than one spot hidden at the same time? The possibilities are endless. Save a copy and start fiddling with the code.

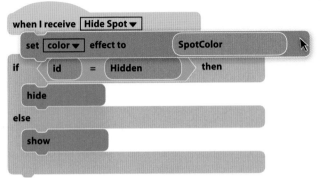

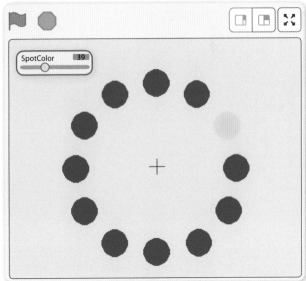

△ **Color controls**

To find out which colors make the illusion strongest, create a new variable called "SpotColor" and add a slider to the stage. Add a "set color effect" block to the sprite's code under the "when I receive" block. Run the project and try different colors. Which ones work best? Does the magic spot change color, too?

■ ■ **TRY THIS**

Speed it up

Try adding a new variable, called "Delay", to set the speed of the magic spot. You'll need to add these two blocks to the code—see if you can figure out where to put them. Right-click (or control/shift-click) on the variable on the stage and choose "slider". Does the illusion still work if you slow it down?

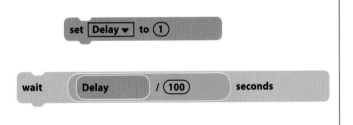

Spiral-o-tron

It's easy to use Scratch's Pen feature to create amazing visual effects, such as this multicolored spinning spiral. If your computer has a microphone, you can adapt the project to make the spiral react to sound.

You can use a microphone to make the spiral move to the music!

How it works

There are many types of spirals, but this project paints a very simple one. Just take a step, turn 10 degrees to your right, take two steps, turn 10 degrees to your right, take three steps, and so on.

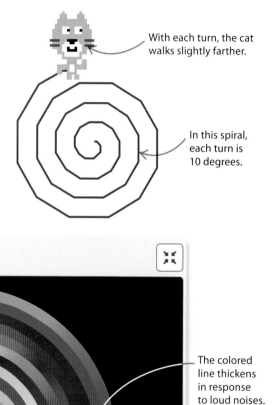

With each turn, the cat walks slightly farther.

In this spiral, each turn is 10 degrees.

This project looks best in full-screen mode.

The colored line thickens in response to loud noises.

The spiral is drawn using the Scratch pen.

Build the spiral

This project shows you how to use Scratch's pen to create fast-moving, interactive effects. Follow the steps below to build a simple spiral first. You'll need to add the Pen extension like you did in previous projects.

1 Start a new project. Delete the cat sprite and click on the paint symbol ✏ in the sprites menu. You don't need to draw a sprite since it's just a guide for the pen. Call the sprite "Spiral".

2 Now, turn the stage black to make the spiral stand out. Click on the backdrop's paint symbol ✏ in the lower right of Scratch. Pick black in the paint editor and use the fill tool to create a solid black backdrop. Make sure you are in Bitmap mode.

Use the fill tool to color the backdrop.

3 The project needs lots of variables. Select the spiral sprite and create the following variables: "Repeats", "DrawLength", "DrawLengthIncrease", "TurnAngle", and "StartDirection". Uncheck their boxes so they don't appear on the stage.

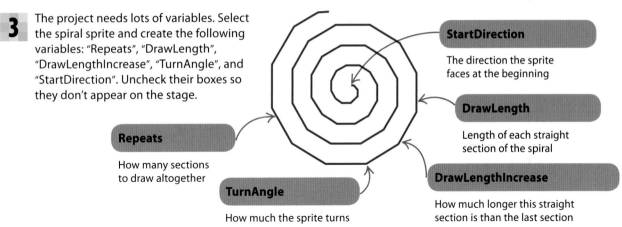

StartDirection

The direction the sprite faces at the beginning

DrawLength

Length of each straight section of the spiral

DrawLengthIncrease

How much longer this straight section is than the last section

Repeats

How many sections to draw altogether

TurnAngle

How much the sprite turns

4 Now create a custom block to draw a spiral. Select My Blocks and then click on "Make a Block".

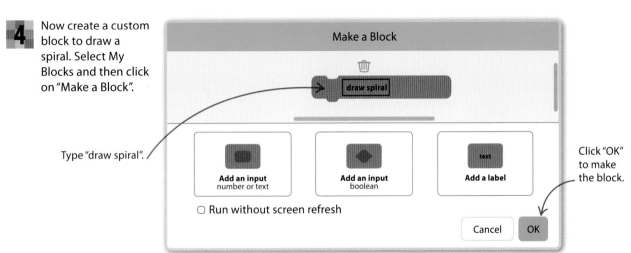

Make a Block

draw spiral

Type "draw spiral".

Add an input
number or text

Add an input
boolean

text
Add a label

☐ Run without screen refresh

Cancel   OK

Click "OK" to make the block.

5 You will now see the "define draw spiral" header in the code area. Add the following code to it. Read through the Scratch blocks and think about the steps. Don't run the project yet because there isn't any code to trigger the new block.

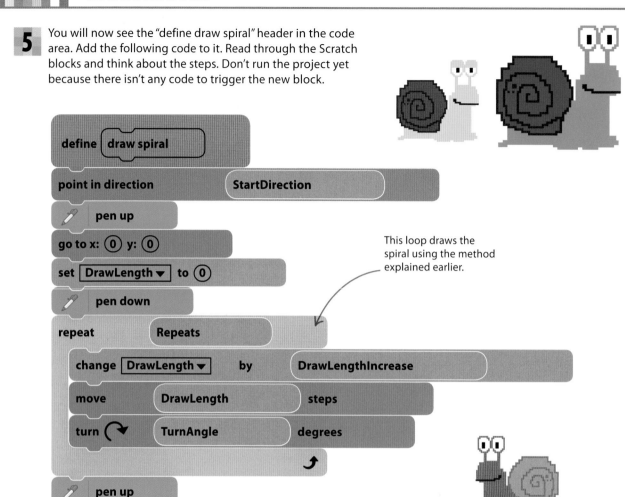

define draw spiral

point in direction StartDirection

pen up

go to x: 0 y: 0

set DrawLength ▾ to 0

pen down

This loop draws the spiral using the method explained earlier.

repeat Repeats

change DrawLength ▾ by DrawLengthIncrease

move DrawLength steps

turn ↻ TurnAngle degrees

pen up

6 Now add the main code to set up the variables and trigger the "draw spiral" block.

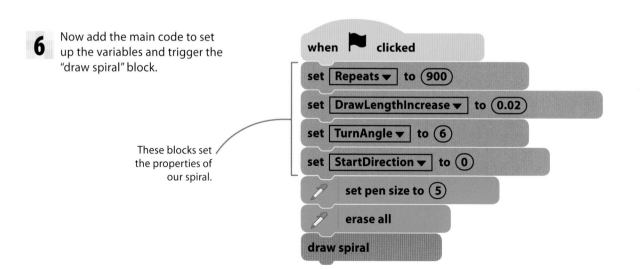

when ⚑ clicked

set Repeats ▾ to 900

set DrawLengthIncrease ▾ to 0.02

set TurnAngle ▾ to 6

set StartDirection ▾ to 0

These blocks set the properties of our spiral.

set pen size to 5

erase all

draw spiral

7 Run the project. A spiral like this will appear. It will take around 30 seconds to draw.

Spin the spiral

To make the spiral spin, Scratch will draw it repeatedly, each time in a new position. To make this happen quickly, you need to use a special trick to run blocks faster.

8 The spiral takes a long time to draw because Scratch redraws the whole stage every time you add a new straight-line section to the spiral. You can set the custom block to not redraw the spiral until it's finished. To do this, right-click on the "define" block and choose "Edit".

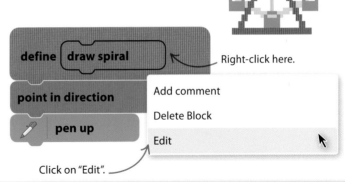

Right-click here.

Click on "Edit".

9 Now, check the box labeled "Run without screen refresh".

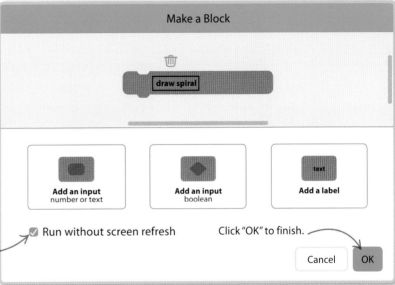

Click here for fast drawing.

Click "OK" to finish.

10 Now, run the project, and the spiral will appear so quickly that you won't see it happen. The next trick is to keep redrawing the spiral in different positions so it appears to spin. Add a new variable called "SpinSpeed", uncheck its box, and change the main code to look like this.

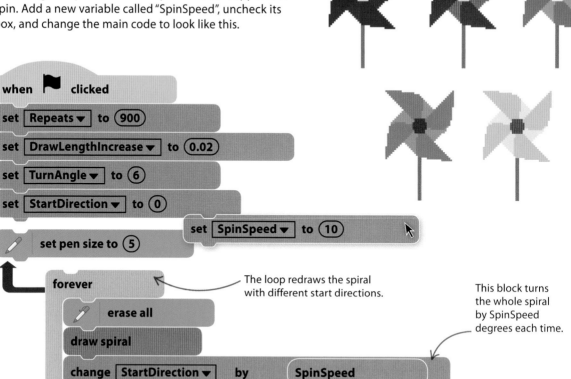

```
when ⚑ clicked
set Repeats ▼ to (900)
set DrawLengthIncrease ▼ to (0.02)
set TurnAngle ▼ to (6)
set StartDirection ▼ to (0)
        set SpinSpeed ▼ to (10)
🖊 set pen size to (5)

forever
    🖊 erase all
    draw spiral
    change StartDirection ▼ by   SpinSpeed
```

The loop redraws the spiral with different start directions.

This block turns the whole spiral by SpinSpeed degrees each time.

Click here for full-screen mode.

11 Run the project, and watch the spiral spin. Try switching to full-screen mode for a hypnotic effect. If you stare at the center for a while and then look away, you might see things ripple weirdly for a moment—an optical illusion.

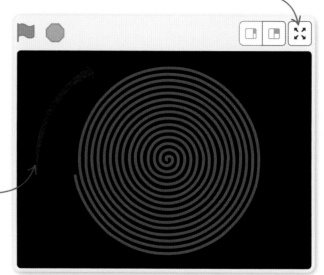

The whole spiral spins clockwise.

Add some color

The pen color can be controlled to create some amazing effects. Simple changes to the code create patterns like the one shown here.

12 Add another variable: "ColorChange". Then change the code as shown here, and run it to see the new colorful spiral.

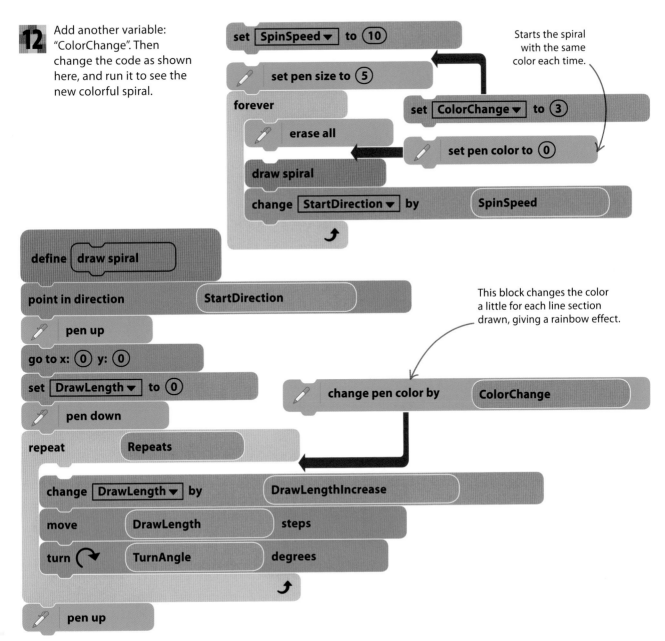

set SpinSpeed to 10

set pen size to 5

forever
  erase all
  draw spiral
  change StartDirection by SpinSpeed

Starts the spiral with the same color each time.

set ColorChange to 3

set pen color to 0

define draw spiral

point in direction StartDirection

pen up

go to x: 0 y: 0

set DrawLength to 0

pen down

repeat Repeats
  change DrawLength by DrawLengthIncrease
  move DrawLength steps
  turn TurnAngle degrees

pen up

This block changes the color a little for each line section drawn, giving a rainbow effect.

change pen color by ColorChange

Move to the music

If your computer has a microphone, you can make the spiral react to sounds and music. You'll need to use special blocks that detect and measure sound volume.

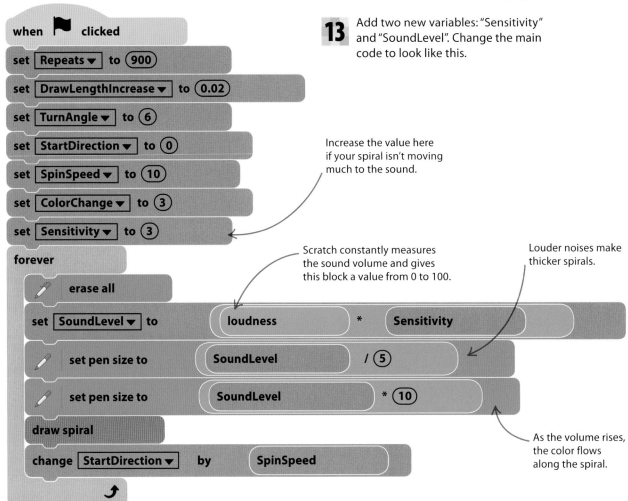

```
when 🏴 clicked
set Repeats ▼ to (900)
set DrawLengthIncrease ▼ to (0.02)
set TurnAngle ▼ to (6)
set StartDirection ▼ to (0)
set SpinSpeed ▼ to (10)
set ColorChange ▼ to (3)
set Sensitivity ▼ to (3)
forever
    erase all
    set SoundLevel ▼ to ( loudness * Sensitivity )
    set pen size to ( SoundLevel / (5) )
    set pen size to ( SoundLevel * (10) )
    draw spiral
    change StartDirection ▼ by ( SpinSpeed )
```

13 Add two new variables: "Sensitivity" and "SoundLevel". Change the main code to look like this.

Increase the value here if your spiral isn't moving much to the sound.

Scratch constantly measures the sound volume and gives this block a value from 0 to 100.

Louder noises make thicker spirals.

As the volume rises, the color flows along the spiral.

14 Run the project and play some music or sing near your computer. Scratch will ask you to use your microphone—it's OK to click "yes." The spiral will dance to the music!

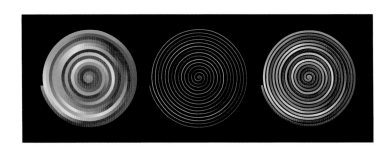

Hacks and tweaks

Don't be afraid to change the variables or other numbers in the code to see what happens. You can also add slider controls to experiment with the look and motion of the spiral.

▽ Sliders

If you show the control variables on the stage, you can right-click and add sliders to them. These allow you to experiment with different values while the project is running.

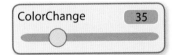

▽ Presets

If you use your sliders to make a spiral you really like, write down all the values and then create a "preset" to set those values at the touch of a key.

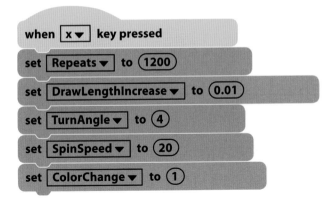

▽ Hiders

You can add code blocks like these to show and hide your sliders when you hit certain keys. That way they won't spoil the view!

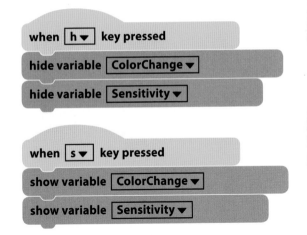

· · ■ TRY THIS

Sound reaction

You can have a lot of fun in other projects making sprites react to sound. Check the "loudness" block to see the volume displayed on the stage. Try giving code blocks like these to some sprites or invent your own code blocks.

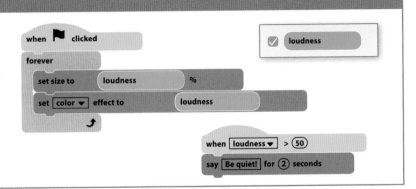

What next?

Next steps

After working through this book, your knowledge of Scratch should be strong enough to take you to new places. Here's some advice on taking your coding skills to the next level, as well as a few suggestions on where to find inspiration for your own projects.

Exploring Scratch

The Scratch website **www.scratch.mit.edu** is a great place to see other people's work and share your own projects. Click "Explore" at the top of the website to view projects that other Scratchers have shared.

There are lots of projects on the Scratch website. Click here to see what great stuff you can find.

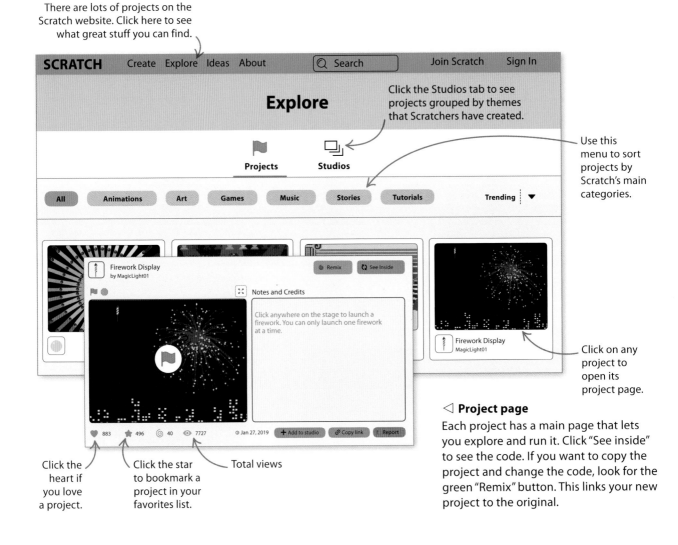

Click the Studios tab to see projects grouped by themes that Scratchers have created.

Use this menu to sort projects by Scratch's main categories.

Click on any project to open its project page.

Click the heart if you love a project.

Click the star to bookmark a project in your favorites list.

Total views

◁ **Project page**
Each project has a main page that lets you explore and run it. Click "See inside" to see the code. If you want to copy the project and change the code, look for the green "Remix" button. This links your new project to the original.

▷ Sharing

To share one of your projects with other Scratchers, open the project and click the "Share" button at the top of Scratch. Anyone can find your project once you've shared it. You can also see how many fellow Scratchers have tried your projects, and people can "favorite" and "love" your project, too.

Making your own projects

Scratch is a great playground for trying out your own coding ideas. Open up a new project and see where your computer mouse takes you.

▽ Doodling

Scratch is designed to make experimenting easy. Just add a sprite you like, and create some fun code blocks like these. Maybe turn on the pen to see what loopy pattern your sprite makes. Play with variables and add sliders so you can see their effects immediately.

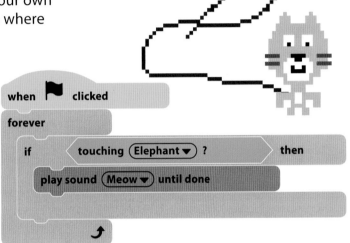

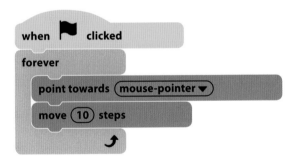

▽ Learn another language

Why not stretch yourself and learn another programming language? Python is easy to get started in, and you'll recognize many of the techniques used in Scratch, like making decisions using "if then" and repeating code with loops.

▽ Have fun!

Programming can be great fun. Working with others and sharing your projects will really help your coding develop. Why not join or start a coding club at your school or local library? Or get together with friends who like Scratch and have a coding party where you can work on themed projects together.

```
if a == 2:
    print("Hello!")
else:
    print("Goodbye!")
```

Scratch   Python

Glossary

algorithm
A set of step-by-step instructions that perform a task. Computer programs are based on algorithms.

animation
Changing pictures quickly to create the illusion of movement.

backpack
A storage area in Scratch that allows you to copy things between projects.

bitmap graphics
Computer drawings stored as a grid of pixels. Compare with *vector graphics*.

block
An instruction in Scratch that can be joined to other blocks to build code.

Boolean expression
A statement that is either true or false, leading to two possible outcomes. Boolean blocks in Scratch are hexagonal instead of rounded.

branch
A point in a program where two different options are available, such as the "if then else" block in Scratch.

bug
A coding error that makes a program behave in an unexpected way.

call
To use a function, procedure, or subprogram. A custom block in Scratch is a call to the "define" code with the same name.

clone
A fully functioning copy of a sprite that can move and run code blocks on its own, separate from the original sprite.

code
A stack of instruction blocks under a header block that are run in order.

condition
A "true or false" statement used to make a decision in a program. See also *Boolean expression*.

coordinates
A pair of numbers that pinpoint an exact spot on the stage. Usually written as (x, y).

costume
The picture a sprite shows on the stage. Rapidly changing a sprite's costume can create an animation.

data
Information, such as text, symbols, or numbers.

debug
To look for and correct errors in a program.

directory
A place to store files to keep them organized.

event
Something a computer program can react to, such as a key being pressed or the mouse being clicked.

execute
See *run*

export
To send something to the computer from Scratch, such as a sprite or a whole project saved as a computer file.

file
A collection of data stored with a name.

fractal
A pattern or shape that looks the same when you zoom in or out, such as the shape of a cloud, a tree, or a cauliflower.

function
Code that carries out a specific task, working like a program within a program. Also called a procedure, subprogram, or subroutine.

global variable
A variable that can be changed and used by any sprite in a project.

gradient (color)
Moving smoothly from one color to another, like the sky during a beautiful sunset.

graphics
Visual elements on a screen that are not text, such as pictures, icons, and symbols.

GUI
The GUI, or graphical user interface, is the name for the buttons and windows that make up the part of the program you can see and interact with.

hack
An ingenious change to code that makes it do something new or simplifies it. (Also, accessing a computer without permission.)

hardware
The physical parts of a computer that you can see or touch, such as wires, the keyboard, and the screen.

header block
A Scratch block that starts a bit of code, such as the "when green flag clicked" block. Also known as a hat block.

import
To bring something in from outside Scratch, such as a picture or sound clip from the computer's files.

index number
A number given to an item in a list.

input
Data that is entered into a computer. Keyboards, mice, and microphones can all be used to input data.

integer
A whole number. An integer does not contain a decimal point and is not written as a fraction.

interface
See *GUI*

library
A collection of sprites, costumes, or sounds that can be used in Scratch programs.

list
A collection of items stored in a numbered order.

local variable
A variable that can be changed by only one sprite. Each copy or clone of a sprite has its own separate version of the variable.

loop
A part of a program that repeats itself, removing the need to type out the same piece of code multiple times.

memory
A computer chip, inside a computer, that stores data.

message
A way to send information between sprites.

network
A group of interconnected computers that exchange data. The internet is a giant network.

operating system (OS)
The program that controls everything on a computer, such as Windows, macOS, or Linux.

operator
A Scratch block that uses data to work something out, such as checking whether two values are equal or adding two numbers together.

output
Data that is produced by a computer program and viewed by the user.

particle effect
A visual effect in which lots of small patterns move in an organized way to create a larger pattern. Particle effects in Scratch usually use clones.

physics
The science of how things move and affect each other. Including physics is often important in simulations and games—for example, to create realistic gravity.

pixel art
A drawing made of giant pixels or blocks, mimicking the appearance of graphics in early computer games.

pixels
The colored dots on a screen that make up graphics.

procedure
Code that carries out a specific task, working like a program within a program. Also called a function, subprogram, or subroutine.

program
A set of instructions that a computer follows in order to complete a task.

programming language
A language that is used to give instructions to a computer.

project
Scratch's name for a program and all the sprites, sounds, and backdrops that go with it.

Python
A popular programming language created by Guido van Rossum. Python is a great language to learn after Scratch.

random
A function in a computer program that allows unpredictable outcomes. Useful when creating games.

run
The command to make a program start.

Scratcher
Someone who uses Scratch.

server
A computer that stores files accessible via a network.

simulation
A realistic imitation of something. A weather simulator might re-create the action of wind, rain, and snow.

software
Programs that run on a computer and control how it works.

sprite
A picture on the stage in Scratch that code blocks can move and change.

stage
The screenlike area of the Scratch interface in which projects run.

statement
The smallest complete instruction a programming language can be broken down into.

string
A series of characters. Strings can contain numbers, letters, or symbols.

subprogram or subroutine
Code that carries out a specific task, working like a program within a program. Also called a function or procedure.

turbo mode
A way of running Scratch projects that makes the code work much faster than normal. You can switch turbo mode on and off by holding the shift key as you click the green flag.

tweak
A small change made to something to make it work better or differently.

variable
A place to store data that can change in a program, such as the player's score. A variable has a name and a value.

vector graphics
Computer drawings stored as collections of shapes, making them easier to change. Compare with *bitmap graphics*.

Index

Page numbers in **bold** refer to main entries.

Acknowledgments

Dorling Kindersley would like to thank Caroline Hunt and Steph Lewis for proofreading; Helen Peters for the index; Sean Ross for help with Scratch; Ira Pundeer for editorial assistance; Nishwan Rasool for picture research assistance; Abhijit Dutta, Priyanka Sharma, and Mark Silas for code testing; and Vishal Bhatia for pre-production assistance.

Jon Woodcock would like to thank all his code clubbers over the years for teaching him how to think in Scratch; and Matty and Amy for all their questions.

Scratch is developed by the Lifelong Kindergarten Group at MIT Media Lab. See **http://scratch.mit.edu**

The publisher would like to thank the following for their kind permission to reproduce their photographs:

(Key: a-above; b-below/bottom; c-center; f-far; l-left; r-right; t-top)

134 123RF.com: Jacek Chabraszewski (b); **Dreamstime.com**: Pavel Losevsky (b/background); **163 Corbis**: Trizeps Photography / photocuisine (cra); **NASA**: (cr); **Science Photo Library**: SUSUMU NISHINAGA (crb); **173 NOAA**: (tr)

All other images © Dorling Kindersley Limited